Shadows in Winter

Library of Modern Jewish Literature

Leah and Aderet at Morro Rock

Shadows in Winter

A Memoir of Love and Loss

EITAN FISHBANE

With a Foreword by Leon R. Kass, M.D.

SYRACUSE UNIVERSITY PRESS

First Edition 2011

11 12 13 14 15 16   6 5 4 3 2 1

∞ The paper used in this publication meets the minimum requirements
of the American National Standard for Information Sciences—Permanence
of Paper for Printed Library Materials, ANSI Z39.48-1992.

For a listing of books published and distributed by Syracuse University
Press, visit our Web site at SyracuseUniversityPress.syr.edu.

ISBN: 978-0-8156-0989-6

Library of Congress Cataloging-in-Publication Data

Fishbane, Eitan P., 1975–

  Shadows in winter : a memoir of love and loss / Eitan Fishbane. — 1st ed.

     p. cm. — (Library of modern Jewish literature)

  ISBN 978-0-8156-0989-6 (cloth : alk. paper) 1. Fishbane, Eitan P.,
1975– 2. Fishbane, Leah Levitz. 3. Wives—Death—Psychological
aspects. 4. Grief. 5. Bereavement—Psychological aspects. 6. Loss
(Psychology) I. Title.

  BF575.G7F555 2011

  296.7'6092—dc23   2011025266

Manufactured in the United States of America

Illustrations

Contents

Eitan Fishbane is Assistant Professor of Jewish Thought at the Jewish Theological Seminary in New York. He is the author or editor of several books, including *The Sabbath Soul: Mystical Reflections on the Transformative Power of Holy Time* and *Jewish Mysticism and the Spiritual Life: Classical Texts, Contemporary Reflections*.

For Aderet, with love

I will remember for you

Foreword

Leon R. Kass, M.D.*

To say yes to love is to say yes to loss. To give one's heart is to risk having it broken, if not sooner, then eventually through death. When death comes, the more deeply we have loved, the more deeply do we grieve. As C. S. Lewis put it, "The pain I feel now is the happiness I had before. That's the deal."

For those still in mourning, such words of wisdom bring little comfort. But for those whose soul mate is snatched away early on their journey, there can be no such "deal," and their grief defies any such measure. "The overwhelming pain I feel now is also the happiness I am denied, is also the happiness we never got to have."

Who can speak truly to such grief? What can young love lost say to itself—and to the life and love that are lost? This book is one man's attempt at heartfelt, heartbroken, and honest speech.

On February 27, 2007, Leah Levitz Fishbane was brought to Hackensack University Medical Center because of persistent headaches, recent vomiting, and resulting dehydration. Age thirty-two, the wife of Eitan Fishbane,

*Committee on Social Thought, University of Chicago

Leah was eight weeks pregnant with the couple's second child. In love since their student days at Brandeis and married in 1999 (my wife and I danced at their joyous wedding), Leah and Eitan were a couple that did honor to the Great Matchmaker who, it is said, sends lovers "leaping over the mountains" to their beloveds. Nine months earlier, they had bought and settled into their first house, in Teaneck, New Jersey. After several years teaching elsewhere (one year at Carleton College and three years at Hebrew Union College in Los Angeles), Eitan, a scholar of Jewish mysticism, theology, and ethics, was newly appointed—and welcomed with great enthusiasm—as an assistant professor at the Jewish Theological Seminary in New York, where a promising career awaited him. Leah, herself at work on a doctoral dissertation in American Jewish history, was thriving, as was their daughter, Aderet, the object of her mother's devotion. Not yet four years old, Aderet was—is—any parent's dream: lively and energetic, warm and affectionate, imaginative and playful, articulate, sensitive, and smart, smart already in more than childish ways about the things that matter. As it had been in Los Angeles, so now in Teaneck Leah and Eitan's home was becoming a hub for family and friends, especially on Shabbat, where all who gathered were carried upward by their grace, warmth, and spirituality. A new career; a new home in a welcoming community; a new child on the way—a beautiful life, now bursting into full flower.

Within forty-eight hours, beautiful Leah, full of life, had disappeared, first into deep coma, then altogether— the victim of a hitherto undiagnosed brain tumor, which, with the surrounding swelling, compressed the brain stem and cut off respiration and all signs of life. Without warning, without time even to anticipate the worst, a precious life is extinguished, a soul is stolen away before its full glory could be lived and seen, before its blessings could be bestowed fully on those whose lives she had touched and would yet touch. Left behind are precious lives in tatters: her father and her mother, having buried their daughter; her young daughter bereft of her mother; and her beloved Eitan, so recently a bridegroom, overnight a widower beyond anguish.

Out of the depths of his sorrow, Eitan, in the weeks that followed Leah's death, turned to poetry and took up his own pen—to try to give voice to his inexpressible sorrow, to search for his absent Leah, to pick up the shards of his broken life, to tell himself the truth about what he has lost, what he is feeling, and about what life now means to him and to his beloved Aderet. Days turn into weeks, and weeks into months, but the emptiness remains, as does the need to understand and to find meaning in meaning's absence. As "life goes on," waves of sadness and sacred memories sneak up on him, bringing the missing Leah into loving presence, only to pierce the heart because she must now forever live for him only in memory.

Eitan's memoir, written steadily over the first five months after Leah's death, is less a conventional portrait of the lost beloved, more an account of life lived with love lost, through which the missing Leah emerges from the shadows, reflected in the pools of sorrow her departure has created, and the power of her person is revealed through

Eitan's moving words of longing and remembrance. Memories fade in and out, tears come and go, the details of daily life are filled with Leah's absent presence—not only for Eitan but also for little Aderet, to whose deeds and speech he also gives poignant and powerful voice. This is not an account written retrospectively in tranquillity—"Put it away for a while, when you have more perspective, and it will be easier to read"—but intensely, truly, in the midst of the whirlwind.

As a result, Eitan's memoir is wrenching, the sentiments raw, and the words sear the soul. But, for this very reason, this intense story of love and grief has the singular virtue of being honest to lived experience, and for that it deserves our attention. In an age when grief is so often treated as a problem to be solved rather than a burden to be borne, and when everybody preaches the power of "positive thinking," readers will be grateful for this noble demonstration of what it means deeply and truly to grieve—and with dignity. Best of all, we will applaud this compelling example of honoring the memory of one's beloved by giving true and beautiful poetic voice to what only a deeply loving soul can feel and know in the midst of, and through, his grief.

Shadows in Winter

1

Finding the Words

Now, after all these many years, poetry returns. *And it comes from a place inside that you had wanted me to find again*—quiet while the loneliness had receded. But I am cut open, and I bleed and bleed.

The eye of memory is a strange thing: to try to evoke in thought, and then how much harder in words, that elusive power of a presence—that resistance against the flow of time, a reality that never had to be re-created, because it *just was*. But still I try—for memories and traces are all she is now.

Words in the dark: like blazing lanterns in the night-
forest.
And then silence: trying to speak in the place of the
speechless.

"What happened to her is tragic." *Tragic.* The words of the neurosurgeon still ring clearly in my ear, and the haze of those hours comes back to me again—my own private lamentation.

> *Lonely sits the city*
> *once great with people!*
> *She that was great among nations*
> *Is become like a widow.*

Bitterly she weeps in the night,
Her cheek wet with tears.

People are still roundabout me, but I am alone.

Alone.

At that point we didn't expect anything different; not after two days of feeling the shadows creep in, of hearing one doctor after another deliver the message that there was little hope to hold on to.

"Right now all we can do is pray for a miracle," said one of the physicians who had been with us since the nightmare began on Tuesday morning. He said it with great compassion.

Lying on that hospital bed in the ICU, the respirator inhaling and exhaling for her, was Leah—the center and anchor of my life. Sweet love, she lay there so helpless and so gentle, and there was nothing I could do to stop the collapse of our life together, happening right before my eyes.

Hands laid at her sides, placed there by the nurses. I almost think she is sitting at that angle deliberately, her arms set out in calm composure. Until the blanket shifts and her hand slips uncontrolled. But they are still her hands. Warm. Soft. Holding her hand I can almost feel the familiar squeeze of her palm, the closing of her fingers in mine. I am still waiting for her to open her eyes, to whisper hoarsely to me: "Eitee . . . bring me some cold water . . . Eitee, my throat is so dry . . ." And the other half of me expects to hear the sound of her healthy voice, familiar as my own blood, as close as the inside of my own head.

So many memories. A thousand moments that circle now through the wheels of my mind like gleaming leaves in late autumn—floating through the air in waves, and the new chill that bears them whispers of the coming winter. Suddenly I feel hollowed out inside. She can't put her hand on my heart, or hold me tightly to her chest. She can't bring me back from the edges of my worry and my fear to tell me that we will be all right after all. She was slipping from me, and with her, the whole of my life was slipping too.

2

Lines in a Portrait

I watch her in this space of shadows and dissolving time. And through the prism of the luminal Beyond, I can see the place where hope and memory meet, where the shape of who she was in life is elevated to a new clarity.

Lifting her image to the light of deliberate memory, the first thing I see is her gentleness: the complete way that she was.

So here it is: I am stunned by how quickly the ordinary fabric of life can be ripped apart.

Maybe that's why it's so hard for me to really see her as an absence, because she was always so present and *real* in so many moments—all those times when I myself was struggling for the same measure. When I think back on it now, as hard as it is to get any perspective on the shape of a life shared, I realize that it was her unpretentious playfulness and pure sweetness that drew me to her back then, and that was our stable anchor on the wild sea path of living.

That is how I want to remember her best: the contagious smile and the affection that she didn't hold back; the patience and the love; the sparkle in her face when she lay on the carpet with our daughter as she was learning to speak and to walk. She would take me in and shelter me; she would be the receiver for the confessions and the secrets of intimacy.

Time passes against my will; memories take on a life of their own. Now it is different: now we are fragments of a story that yearn for reunion. A reunion in the telling.

We build our lives knowing that things will end, that they may end suddenly and harshly. (Isn't that what purchasing insurance represents?) But who really believes that it will happen? Careers, homes, marriages—we enter into their shelter, never quite accepting how fragile they really are. Like the bridges that are constructed over rivers, or the towers that stand above cities: not until the moment of their sudden collapse is it ever imaginable. And then, in the flash of an instant, it's all gone: the security we relied on, the world we knew. To feel the impact of the sudden—it is to witness the disappearance of all that was taken for granted in our lives.

3

On the Edge of the Abyss

There are the little things we talked about doing around the house—a new tub in the bathroom, a new floor in the kitchen. The gliding rocker that Leah wanted to put in the alcove of our bedroom, by the window, for when the baby would need soothing and milk—the baby whose dreamed potential died along with Leah in its tiny eight-week state of development. The heartbeat we had seen together with excitement before we ever imagined that this would be our fate.

Only a week before.

I can still see the handwritten sign posted above her bed in the ICU: "Patient is pregnant."

As if that mattered now.

Mother and fetus traveling together down the grim road of endings.

And there is Aderet.
Four years old, filled with wonder and questions.

Leah took such joy in every moment of Aderet's growth, every new gesture and expression, every milestone that she captured on the digital camera.

I recently came across those videotapes.
I read her handwriting on the labels:

Aderet, 18–32 months
Aderet's 2nd Birthday Party

They were waiting to be rediscovered in a bedroom
drawer—and I anticipate what it will be to hear Leah's
voice again as it was captured by the recording device.
Will it be different than I remember it? Will it bring back
the flood of life and its fleeting moments?

∽

Months later I do hear that voice, I do see her laughing and
moving and appearing to live still. She speaks to Aderet
in the time out of time that we watch. Aderet asks: "Can
Imma see me through the TV?" And she giggles with pleasure at seeing her mother again. It doesn't matter that it is
the trick of machines—for captured here is that unrecover-
able voice, that smile that has been erased from the world.
And so Leah's voice calls out from the Great Beyond: in
the years to come this too will be Aderet's memory—the
sound of her mother playing with her from a time before
remembrance is retained.

∽

Looking back at the still-frame pictures, I can see Leah's
eye on the other side of that lens—her soul-spark shimmer-
ing there, defusing all anxiety and anger in the calm of kind
eyes. And it was her eyes that were at the center of her end
in this world: hour after hour, lights shining on her pupils,

the touch of cold water on her held-open spheres, the doctors looking for any sign of brain function. Any sign.

She will not see our little girl grow, learn to read, learn to ride a bike.

All the beauty that has been stolen from her. And the memories that Aderet has—will they fade entirely? Will they dissolve into the unstoppable passage of time? I don't know if anyone really remembers life in that distant recess of early childhood, or if what we recall is mostly the composite of narratives we are told and the pictures that remain. What will she remember of her mother and the devotion with which Leah surrounded her for those four years? Will all the details be held only in the transmission she receives from me? Will her mind's eye become dominated by the *emotion* of memory, instead of by the particularities of remembrance? The idea that the immediacy of her memory will fade strikes me like a knife in the heart: for how can such an immensity of love ever be forgotten?

And my words—all of them that were to come, and all that were as yet unspoken—they are swallowed into the black hole of unrealized time. It's not just the loneliness— though that in itself is pretty much unbearable—it's this dark emptiness, deep in my chest, and the abyss of all that was anticipated. Little by little, I notice her handwriting on notes scattered through the house, items in the pantry that only I know she bought at the market, pictures hung on the walls reflecting the placement of her hands. There are the reminders and appointments written into the calendar in her distinctive hand—ethereal traces of days she anticipated, but would never see. As time moves forward, as we pass through those foreseen days, I can feel the evanescent markers of her presence.

The nights fall in with their heavy force, and I am awakened by the voice of my little girl: "Abba, I'm having a bad dream."

Three times, just this night. I lie next to her and stroke her head—she holds her picture of Imma tightly to her chest.

> I'm feeling Imma's *keppie*, and I'm smelling Imma's hair smell. Abba—I miss my Imma.
>
> I know, sweetheart—I do too.
>
> But, Abba, Imma's alive in my heart and in my room, right? 'Cause that's where Imma would sit on my bed.

I don't know what to say. *Not really.* So I lie next to my baby girl until I gradually hear her breathing turn to sleep. It's only then—lying in her room so still—that I can see the shadows return to me.

I am now the bearer of her bad dreams.

4

Daydreams

Sun is streaming through the family room windows. I've recently discovered how much sunlight comes in on the first floor—we used to keep the shades down for privacy, but ever since shivah ended it has been comforting to see the broad panes of glass filled with sun. And it was surprising to feel the brightness of winter light in North Jersey. Even while the freezing winds of early March whistled and thumped, the shimmer of morning sun could bring my mood back—a little reminder of the California glow, of gleaming mornings and slow late afternoons.

At 3:30 or 4:00 we might start up the car—*you reassuring me that the chapter I was working on would wait, but precious time together wouldn't*—a bag thrown over her back, packed with all the little essentials that I am only now really aware of. Sunscreen and hats, water and an array of snacks for Aderet, and off we would drive—fifteen minutes on the 10 West to Santa Monica. Walks on the pathway along Ocean Boulevard, the row of palms bracing the rich blue: bright and clear in my memory. And then there were days when a fog was draped over the pier—concealing the Pacific, the low mountains of Malibu waiting as invitation in the distance.

Those were the magical hours—the otherworldly on California time. Evening tide and twilight coming. The sun

in descent, melting on the water: the slow dissolve of earth
and sea into the fluid of night. A full spectrum revealed,
brilliant and molten. Colors distinct and then merging:
rose and magenta, orange-fire and lilac—a mulberry wine
mixed and withdrawn, filling us like an open glass and
pouring out again into the darkness all around.

Pushing Aderet's stroller over the cobblestone of the
Third Street Promenade—the outdoor performers present
like a memory resurfaced, echoes of our walking in Jerusalem all those years ago. Broad walkways and roaming
families. It was a clean, sweet smell—the wondrous blend
of dry Mojave Desert air and the elixir of coastal winds—
the allure of the LA basin and its cradle of dreams.

*You held my hand, our fingers interlaced. We shared a warm drink; we
bought Aderet a special toy.*

Leah's playground would be Williams-Sonoma or Sur
la Table: the gourmet kitchen stores where she could run
her hands along the various fancy implements like a kid
in a toy store. And there she would dreamily contemplate
the kitchen we would have one day when money wasn't
so tight. But for now we would be content with the glazed
ceramic mugs, those that still greet me when I come to
take my morning coffee.

From there we would make our way down to the pier,
with the bright lights of the carousel and the Ferris wheel,
the portraitists drawing passersby for a few dollars, the
man hawking T-shirts and sunglasses, the comfort of sharing the wooden beams of the walkway with the hundreds
of other strangers breathing in the sea air—the perfectly

private located right in the middle of a public thorough-
fare. Those were hours when the cares of ordinary time
would recede; there were only the three of us.

And there were the nights we went out to the Grove—
that dreamy, open-air mall near Fairfax and Third. Aderet
entranced by "the jumping fountain"—the elaborate dis-
play of water shooting and dancing to lights and big-band
music; a crowd of shoppers and wanderers strolling beside
the fountain and the storefronts. I would put Aderet on my
shoulders (and she giggled with excitement), a family of
three meandering through the pedestrian walkways. Leah
and Aderet at a table, waiting for me to deliver dinner from
the kosher hot dog stand. It was the pleasure of simple
things; now it is the pleasure and the agony of remembering the ordinary moments.

Even as I recall it from some distance—and memory
surfaces as shards of light, disjointed pieces to be recon-
structed—the immediacy of her, of her scent, her sound,
of what she would say to me, it is all eerily present; the
shadows that show themselves convincingly as the *thing
itself*, as the person in life. Death, absence, removal of presence—these categories bear the charge of unreality, of my
disbelief. It can't be: I know if I call to her she'll have to
answer. She can't be far; she can't be that far gone.

∽

*And these windows take me back to the summers we spent on the lake—at
your parents' weekend place in the Pennsylvania woods—mornings
where the lake was in love with the dancing sun, and all of
it was open before us through the tall living room panes.*

Hot, amber-colored coffee in our hands, the slow hours before the sun would be directly overhead, the wind chime rustling, sounding its interlaced bells as a call to meditation—and like the monks and nuns of Plum Village, the bells would bring me back to myself, back to a place of perfect stillness, back to a first innocence before the rhythms of nature.

The door to the porch would be opened wide—the breeze of open space sweeping in the cool of lake water. I recall sitting at the dining room table, a Hebrew text open before me (which one I no longer remember), and there are crisp memories of reading Stegner's *Crossing to Safety*— somewhere during one of those radiant summers. Young couples starting out together on the academic road—the romance of early dreams, the excitement in anticipating all that remains to be done. I remember lying in bed there at the lake, reading Stegner—his representation of the yearning in memory for those moments that end up shaping our lives forever. The fragmentary nature of the way we recall, and yet the romance of its enduring feeling:

Madison. It comes back as broken scenes.

Friendships that have come in and out of our lives— moments remembered, fragments left behind.

A few years later we lived out our own *Crossing to Safety* adventure, as we drove that Subaru wagon through Wisconsin farmland (verdant grass-acres, tilled soil, and roadside fruit stands), on our way to Minnesota and Carleton College. Carleton would be my first academic position—a year that comes back to me now as a flood of memories. Finding my way through the exhilaration and mystery of new teaching; our walks along the pathways of the arboretum in the midglory of spangled autumn; evening dinners at that Indian restaurant in downtown Northfield. Perfectly dim, candlelit in my memory. Shabbat afternoons we would meander through the campus and the residential streets filled with big old homes—our quiet college town for the year. Visits to Dr. G.—the tall, gregarious OB who treated Leah over those many months—memories of feeling the kicks and the hiccups, my hand pressed against her pregnant belly; seeing the sonograms together for the first time; that freezing March night when we drove across town to Northfield Hospital, to the birth of our precious baby girl.

Moments of togetherness; moments of transcendence.

I can feel it with all of my senses—as though I am absorbed back into the realm of dreams—the sleepless midnights, the paths open and alive to us. The 2:00 a.m. feedings: Aderet cradled in my arm and resting on the soft green pillow from the living room couch; she drinks in the milk I have prepared for her, long, deep inhalations—her tiny cheeks moving to the rhythm of her sucking, her wide-open eyes gazing up at me with all the wonder of pure reception and pure giving. The night outside is run through with a dark freeze—it reaches 'round this inside space; it curls its cold breath along the walls and walkways. But the silence of that time feels luminous to me—the hushed embrace and the whisper of new life setting the room to its perfect warmth. The feeding done, I kiss my little child on her face—I lay her down in the bassinet beside our bed, and I crawl in next to Leah. Through her sleep my wife takes hold of my hand and pulls it close. There, in the quiet, the world regains full balance; all my fears are forgotten.

And again I am at the lake—our lake—our place of refuge, our place of calm. I can still feel the motion of the docks on long Shabbat afternoons—the two of us lying on our backs, the sound of the water moving in the wake of far-off boats—each moment opening into eternity now in the eye of memory, the lake aglow from the slowly descending orb.

Those summer evenings come and go from deep inside; body and soul open and close in the glimmer of remembrance.

I think of that house on the lake as a space that holds our memories in the walls, for some palpable marker of us must remain there. Sold years ago, it's now taken on the layers of someone else's experience: but I wonder if places can store up scattered fragments of time, if they can serve as the treasure houses of moments gone by—waiting there to be summoned up to the looking glass of memory, sometimes clear, oftentimes opaque. Are there traces of us, of the soft edges of our summer hours—and will they remain somehow on the wood of that deck, looking out on the water?

5

Longing

The house is strangely quiet. Aderet fell asleep on the couch, and it is 4:30 p.m.—the blanket of Shabbat is slowly approaching. And my chest and stomach feel weighed down—it is an ache that is not like an acute pain, just a lingering heaviness that is at once light from sheer emptiness. My breathing is rapid—like the trembling just before the body collapses in weeping. Suddenly I am conscious of a loneliness that is deep and complete, as though a vital part of my body has been removed—no, ripped away—and whatever anesthetic had been given is now wearing off.

You died on the edge of spring, lilacs unbloomed, the snow still on the ground. So many things unfinished. Still so much love.

The truth is my mind keeps returning to the image of her six feet beneath the earth's surface. Standing over Leah's open grave on that Friday noon—the dismal rain of the early morning having been replaced by a clear and bright sun—I felt the false promise of spring, overtures that would be taken back only days later with the last whip and snap of winter snow. Measure by measure, her space in the ground was filled in as the hole in my heart was torn wider. And then, as now, I could understand why people have been so determined to believe in the reality of a soul, in some form of immortality—any transcendence of these terrifying shadows of death. For what is the essence of a person, and what endures in this lifetime of fleeting moments and images?

I am.
She was.

You always walked together, and now she is gone.

So reads the card of a friend—memories of our years in Boston.

What was bound has come undone: the shattered mirror of lost reflections.

Still your body lies concealed in that graveyard, and though I know what I must teach our daughter, I myself don't know where to go to find you. Against every rational thought in my head, I am filled with sadness at how horribly alone you must be now, at the bottom of all that earth.

I think of how my ninety-two-year-old grandmother cried out after my grandfather died, and we couldn't understand her. Not then.

"But he'll be so cold and lonely there all by himself," she wailed through a pain that I only now understand. "My sweetheart, my sweetheart—I can't leave him there all alone."

Were you cold the other night when it was raining? Does that simple pine box protect you, or are you just surrounded by so much darkness? Is that you under the earth? Or am I right in what I tell Aderet, desperate for the words to console her? Does your spirit live on?

I want to halt time in its tracks. I want to demand that the earth wheel cease its unending spin.

My all. My breath.

My space and my time and every inch of me—to know if it is day or night, the moments seen and those hidden from all others; coming apart, coming undone. Past and future collapsing into memory. My secret midnight moments, holding your soft black dress—there, in the quiet, your scent and self return to me, a time that evaporates and disappears.

∾

Tonight I sit in the soft reading chair that we picked out together for the living room. Aderet is asleep, and the house is once again a chasm of quiet—sometimes a welcome and pensive silence, other times the bottomless abyss of disorientation and fear. Do I still linger in the haze of disbelief? Have I crossed the invisible threshold to become aware of this massive hole inside of me—a heartache that makes me feel like my insides are sinking while the shell of my body floats in a dream-fog on the surface of things?

I hold my favorite mug, filled with hot peppermint tea, laced with honey.

Steam rising like the vapor of life.

I am aware of the warmth, and of the sensation of swallowing.

It fills me, and I exhale.

6

Faith

At a deep level, I cannot really separate her identity from mine. And so her absence leaves me feeling incomplete in the most basic of ways—the rest of me has been removed and buried; I try to understand what it is that I am without her. For more than ten years we defined ourselves in relation to one another—there was no real division between us; the presence of the one was the presence of the other. Consciousness and feeling, regret and hope—all of these and more were filtered through the intimacy of relationship, through the oneness of our selfhood. So what does it mean to untangle that thread-weave of binding and oneness? Can it ever be unbound, untangled?

And where is she? Where is she now?

Four-year-old Aderet intuits this with a depth that frequently leaves me stunned.

"Imma is everywhere, Abba. In my room, in the air—but, Abba, can you reach up to the sky and pull Imma down from heaven for me?"

Part of me wants to try.

But all I can do is pull my little girl in closer as I carry her up the hill for the evening prayers. We stand there with the other mourners, all of them from another generation. Even amid community our experience is solitary.

Whose wife dies at thirty-two? Who loses a mother at age four? We stand within a vast abyss—our screams go unanswered.

> *May God's great name be blessed for ever and ever . . .*
> *May great peace and life from heaven be drawn down onto*
>   *us and onto all of Israel, and let us say: Amen.*
> *He who makes peace in the heavens, He will bring peace*
>   *upon us . . .*

These are the words of the kaddish: the prayer we Jews recite aloud in the daily presence of our community. The words are said as announcement, as reminder; they call our fellow Jews into the momentary awareness of our ongoing condition. But do the words themselves really mean anything to me? Is this the God of *my* faith, or is it merely a relic of an older, outmoded theology—one that we hold on to with the desperate clutch of childhood simplicity?

"Abba, you know what? I think Imma and God are playing checkers together! And when God is gonna make it rain, Imma can say: No, God. I don't want it to rain on my Aderet and my Eitee! And you know what? God listens to her, and it doesn't rain!"

Blessing. Peace. Life. The refrain of my outward grief, my communal grief—words spoken for generations and generations. But these words ring hollow. What peace? And where am I to find blessing and life in all of this? The liturgy refers to God as the Compassionate One, but I see no compassion and no mercy. I want to rewrite the language of the prayers: *He who curses. He who makes war. He who doles*

out death with a merciless hand. This is the refrain of my inward
grief, my private world. And yet the problem of injustice
was never my theological problem. I could never believe
in that kind of God anyway: not in the God of Justice who
controls and destines everything; the God who is portrayed
as the Great King and grand puppeteer of the universe. For
me, God was always more of an animating life force in the
world: the breath that lies at the center of things; the pulse
and lifeblood of the Great All of Being. And so there was
never the presumption that some Hand was guiding the
destinies of life. I think of that image even more so now
when I recall Leah's final passage from the physical realm.
The departure of breath: the withdrawal of life's vital center
and spiritual essence.

But my daughter's speech encapsulates our most basic
religious dilemma, the reason so many feel they have lost
their faith in the wake of tragedy and injustice: "Abba, I'm
mad at God. I'm mad at Him for making Imma die. I'm
gonna hit God, and I'm gonna make him throw up! Are you
mad at God, too, Abba?"

I see that this struggle is instinctual; it's burned into
the psyche even at a young age. But the God of my religious life is not the "Our Father, Our King" of the classical liturgy. I do not believe in a God who is represented
as the ultimate arbiter of cosmic justice, nor as the one
who takes the most precious of young souls to heaven.
These explanations feel shallow to me—they reduce the
complexity and ineffability of living and dying to a child-
like sense of order, of cause and effect. I have always felt
much closer to the idea that God's mysterious presence

is to be found in all the ordinary shadows of worldly life;
that the river of Divinity courses through the body of the
world like the circulation of blood in the human being;
that God is, in the final analysis, the ultimate life-breath
of existence—inseparable from it, and therefore manifest
in all of its beauty and all of its horror. In this way, God is
the great oneness of reality, and we are but the many faces
of that larger radiance. God is not the superhuman figure
that dwells in the transcendent heavens; Divinity is in the
here and now—God is the space within the inextricable
threads of life, the mystery that pulses at the core of our
living and our dying. In the cycles of our being we reflect
the tragedy and the brokenness that are a part of God;
but we also reflect the sublime beauty and the redemption
that is God's presence as well.

I think again about the closing lines of the kaddish:
"May great peace and life from heaven be drawn down
onto us." It is a prayer for peace when the world feels rup-
tured and violent; it is a cry for renewed life when we feel
weakest and most drained of energy. In the darkness, it is
a mantra of hope: please give us the strength to believe
that life is still possible, that we might find some peace in
this place of despair.

7

Descent

We thought it was just a bad run of pregnancy sickness—never imagining that we were entering the final days of your life. Now, in retrospect, I know the tumor was putting increasing pressure on her brain—making her weaker, torturing her with violent headaches and horrible hours of illness. I find myself (against my better judgment) allowing my mind to go down the dangerous road of *what if* and *if only.* The headaches she suffered for nearly ten years—what if we had done more CT scans more recently? Would we have found her invader in time? How is it possible that the best neurologists in Boston, the headache specialists who took no insurance—how could they not have found her killer before he surfaced? Was he not really there inside of her yet? Is this all just a bizarre series of coincidences?

Back in time.
If only.
What happened to her is tragic.

The top of my dresser is still strewn with Leah's medicine bottles, and a scrap of paper survives to remind me of those days of suffering: Zofran—8 p.m., Compazine—2 a.m., Tylenol with Codeine—4 a.m. *And nothing to relieve your pain—not really.* After two days of feeling a bit better (might we actually have a day of reprieve from this horrid pregnancy?), Monday night came—*the beginning of your last fall from this world.* Throwing up blood, pain in her head that she begged me to exorcise, the delirium of sleeplessness—a panic and fear that I had never seen in her before.

> *Please*
> *Please*
> *help . . . me . . .*
> *Get this . . . out . . . of . . . my . . . head . . .*

All of a sudden I am in the middle of complete unreality: Leah lying on the floor of the hospital room, a code team of doctors working on her—Dr. A., the high-risk obstetrics doc, kneeling over her—*finding your pulse, finding your breath.*

"Leah—wake up. Leah, can you hear me?"

He taps her gently on the cheek.

"Give me Thiamine—I need *Thiamine!*"

Another doctor comes in—now there are six of them, and me, cramped into the little bathroom where she passed out in my arms.

"Is she breathing?" the other one asks.

"This is the husband," one of the nurses says, gesturing in my direction.

They have an oxygen mask over her face, which she keeps trying to pull off.

Through delirium, she says:

> *I don't want . . . to be . . . pregnant . . .*
> *I don't . . . want . . .*

If nobody else knows, I know: she very much wanted to have another child; she yearned for a second baby. But the suffering was so great, the pain was wrenching open her soul.

And then:

Where . . . am I . . . ? What's . . . ba-ppen-ing . . . ?

"Come with me, sir—we're going to lift your wife onto a stretcher."

"Is she stabilized?" says another.

"I want her put in the room across from the nurses' station," Dr. A. directs.

"She needs close monitoring. Get an EKG, and put her on a pulse-ox monitor right away. And page cardiology and neurology."

"She's gonna be okay," he says to me with kindness. "We'll figure out what's wrong with her."

Part of me wanted to scream and wail, and the other part felt the glaze of surreality hovering about me, enshrouding the hospital corridors.

What do you think it is? I ask, feeling the world's motion very slowly.

"Still hard to be sure, but it could be her blood sugar. We're gonna need to do some more tests to determine the cause."

And more tests would come.

They took Leah to a new room where she could be closely watched. She was still very disoriented. About twenty minutes before the fainting she had started expressing that confusion.

Where am
I? I don't
know
where . . . I am . . .

Was that the dehydration talking?

Can't you get a neurologist to see her any faster?!

She still knew her name, still recognized me—but her mind was going quickly at that point.

We just didn't know it yet.

Her whole body was restless.

Shortly after they moved her to the new room, I noticed that her right leg was stuck on the grooves of the bed rail. It wouldn't bend to be freed when the nurse and I tried to move it—the leg was completely rigid. She started making a loud sound through her nose and mouth. The nurses checked her chin; her jaw was clamped down tight.

"She's seizing! Call a code—*now!*"

In a matter of seconds the code team was once again at her bedside, an array of physicians, each (it seemed) with a different role and specialty.

"Give me 5 of Ativan!" one of the doctors ordered.

"And let's intubate now—"

"Another dose of Ativan!"

I stood by the door to the room, watching—my heart in my throat.

"Sir, why don't you come with me to a quiet waiting area. We'll come and get you with any new information." I could see their considerable discomfort in having me stand there.

"I'll stay here," I said.

I had to watch—these people were trying to save her, but she was a patient to them. A medical case. *No—someone who loved her had to be there.*

I still thought that I could protect her.

"I'm thinking we're looking at a cerebral edema," one doctor said to another, coming out of the room.

I interrupt. Cerebral edema?

"Yes. That's a swelling of the brain. We just don't know what's causing it yet."

What did they think it could be?

"My hunch is that she's experiencing an extreme fluctuation in her blood-sugar levels. Or it could be an unusual reaction to the medications she is taking. We're just going to have to wait and see."

I didn't know it then, but those moments before the seizure would be the last time I would speak to Leah (at least when she was conscious)—and it was the last she would speak to me. From that instant, she would never regain consciousness. Remembering it now, I wonder what her last thought was before slipping under: Was her mind thinking clearly enough at that point to harbor any organized consciousness, or was it just the moving slides of fleeting perception? Did she intuit that these would be her last moments of awareness and seeing? Was she thinking of Aderet? Was she thinking of me?

A strange daze had begun to settle over me as I watched the doctors and nurses coming and going. At short intervals my cell phone would ring, and I would deliver updates on Leah's condition to members of the family.

"Mr. Fishbane, I have some important forms for you to sign over at the nurses' station."

"What are these?" I ask, barely able to hear any response. My movements are slow.

"Hospital waivers. We need to do a CT scan to see if there's any swelling that might be causing your wife's symptoms. This waiver is necessary since Leah is pregnant . . ."

I look over to Leah's OB doctor, a petite woman who would show me great humanity in the hours that were to follow.

"Is there any reason I should be concerned about signing this?" I ask her.

Funny. I was still thinking about the pregnancy. Still thinking about my Leah as an expecting mom.

"It's absolutely necessary," she reassures me. "Our first priority is to find out what's going on with Leah and to get her better. Afterwards we can reassess the pregnancy."

Afterwards.

I nod and sign the papers.

"We'll take her down for the CAT scan very soon," one of the doctors says to me.

"Is there anything I can get for you?" says a nurse. "Something to drink or to eat?"

But hunger has already left me at that point.

"I would like a little coffee. Do you have any fresh coffee?"

Something to help lift the haze. As if that would come from more caffeine. Or maybe it was just the desire to hold something warm in my hands. To have the security of the regular motion of sipping a hot drink.

And before I know it I am walking alongside the rolling gurney—one of the nurses squeezing air into the manual respirator as we rush down the labyrinth of hospital corridors to radiology. I am directed to an isolated gray plastic chair outside the scan room.

"You can wait here for us," one of the doctors says.

"I can't come inside?" Of course I already know the answer.

"No—I'm sorry. We won't be long, though."

∽

So I wait. Quiet, empty halls. The faint sounds of them working behind the closed doors. Even at that moment I feel reality unfolding outside of myself. As in a dream.

Is this happening?

At what point is Leah going to wake up and relieve me of this terror?

She had scans like this before.

Years before when the headaches began.

But there was never anything alarming in them: just the unlucky fate of chronic headaches. *Just.*

"Feel my forehead," she would say to me. "Do I have a fever?"

"Honey, I just felt it a little while ago—you don't feel warm."

Then she makes that playful sad face—our little game of love. So I sigh and put my palm on her head.

Other times, she says: "Eitee, do you think I'm sick—you know, really sick?"

But how could we have ever imagined?

Waiting here, I think of your softness, I think of your touch. Sitting in the dark of the movie theater—the lights dimming, the music beginning. Holding your hand then I always felt like a kid again. Happy. Content.

I remember nights when my parents would babysit at our little house on Shenandoah Street in LA, and we would head over to Beverly Drive—to Mulberry's, for the best white pizza in town, or to Urth Café across the street, where the atmosphere was a perfect romance, little tables tucked into corners, low candles lit on each one, and an exotic array of teas and pastries. We would stand there for long moments smelling each canister—inhaling the perfume of dried leaves. I can still recall the scent of blackberry—or was it peach?—jasmine, Ceylon, and mint. And of course there was the banana cream pie. Two spoons—and again the rising steam of tea.

Those moments stand like sanctuary now, a quiet set aside deep within. All the secrets we shared on those early nights of Pacific wind—the cool that washed over us as we talked through what seemed important at the time. What frustrated us, what we hoped for—planning for a future that seemed like a broad expanse of adventures and possibilities. Only our togetherness was taken for granted—expectations for Aderet, and wonder about children yet unborn. Of what will come.

Of what will come.

ꝏ

The doors to the CT scan room open; the team of doctors emerges. It is Dr. A. who speaks to me first.

"Mr. Fishbane."

The haze of my waking dreams drifts out and passes over me again.

"The scan shows a large mass in your wife's brain. From the CT we can't tell whether it is a tumor or a bleed, and we'll need to do an MRI to determine that."

Again I am outside of myself, observing the scene in which I am the center figure. The odd sensation of unreality. *Did he actually just say that? Did I imagine the whole thing?* I suddenly understand that each moment of terror on this otherwise ordinary Tuesday has led to this, each step leading us with an inexorable force to the worst-case scenario. Now falling, falling—into the emptiness of the nonexistent, of disbelief, into a story that is not mine. *Not mine . . .*

"So it's bad either way," I hear myself say.

As before, I am not really asking.

"It doesn't look good," Dr. A. replies in a soft voice. "All we can do right now is pray."

He places his hand on my shoulder in a gesture of healing. My chest and abdomen rise and fall with the heaviness of breath.

I feel the blood receding from my face—fear rising slowly in me from an unknown interior space.

I can't believe this is
happening
I can't
believe

I can see how they are all looking at me then—the critical-care specialist, the high-risk obstetrics people, the radiologist. Suddenly I am that person—the recipient of the news the physician dreads delivering, the one standing in the inner circle of tragedy.

∽

The wheel of life as it is known spins, and I am—in an instant—lost and adrift. From the morning to the afternoon—not even a day—from presence to absence, from knowing to unknowing, I reel on the sharp edge of Being.

Now I sit in another waiting area—this one outside the MRI room. First I am debriefed by the technicians—to be sure there is no metal in Leah's body before sending her into the magnetic technology.

I sign more release forms for the hospital.

And then alone again.

Brief moments on the phone where I try to fill in members of the family, where they try to send me their love.

They cry with me.

And then I cry alone.

When the tears come I can feel the threads of my world unraveling—no more barriers, just an abyss of darkness underfoot, like the recurring dream of falling, except this time I don't wake up.

Crying never came easily for me—the feelings there hidden out of sight, in the silence of my insides. *And that always frustrated you—wanting to know I could weep, that I would weep for you, if it ever came to that.*

It has come to that.

"If I ever go, you'd better cry for me," she said to me in her playful way.

Can you see me crying for you now?

There, outside the MRI room, the tears rose in my throat; they pummeled my lungs. My chest and shoulders convulsed; my face was quivering and wet. I couldn't even remember when last I cried. Not like this.

In your time of dying.

The time when memories of the life we had made together burned in my chest, weighed on my breathing.

Dr. R. found me there—your obstetrician with the sweet face—and she did what none of the others could do. She held my left hand in hers, and she cried with me.

"You shouldn't be alone," she kept saying to me.

"You shouldn't be alone."

"I just keep thinking about my little girl," I breathed, barely sounding the words through my choked throat. "I try to imagine her growing up without her mom, and my heart breaks all over again."

"She has *you*," Dr. R. says—her voice also shaking with tears. "She has you."

I smile for a short moment—I am comforted by the presence of this kind person, a person I barely know.

∽

The team of doctors comes out again, this time to confirm that it is indeed a tumor in her brain. They speak gently.

They tell me they have asked the Jewish chaplain to come sit with me.

I feel numbed by the haze that has descended onto me.

"I'm not giving up on her yet," says Dr. H., the critical-care specialist who, less than two days later, would be the one to confirm and pronounce brain death.

"We are moving her to the Medical ICU so that we can monitor the swelling in her brain more closely," one of them tells me.

But I am still waiting to wake up—to be relieved of the nightmare I am living.

That strange sense of dream would stay with me for a good ten days—and it comes back to me still as I look around at my life and wonder where in the world my Leah has gone. Now absence is the deepest and most persistent presence—an all-encompassing consciousness of my nights and days.

8

Beginnings

It was in Boston that we met—at the late shift for dinner at Brandeis—and the Boston area would be our home for nearly ten years. Before Northfield, before Los Angeles—before our return to the East Coast. It's odd to think of my life as divided into its component parts, as made up of so many separate chapters that somehow get woven together, and that take their place in a narrative of any coherence. In their time they feel like mere stepping-stones; in retrospect they become clear markers on the way to what we would become. Our abrupt ending drives me to call up the memories of our beginning. First and last bound together as the bookends of our story.

There was a walk in the woods—early spring, I think, some twelve years ago—through the winding dirt path behind the Sachar Building at Brandeis. Standing on the edge of something great and unknown.

But it was always that day in Gloucester that you remembered. Eating lunch in that dark wood-paneled fish place, and then just sitting in the car across from the restaurant for the rest of the afternoon—hard rain sweeping the windshield and drumming the roof of my old Saab. Talking and holding hands until it was time to eat again. Salmon and risotto for dinner at a place across town—candles on the table, warm orange-painted walls, secrets shared in a space of unknowns and expectations. Time out of time. Place out of place.

There were late nights of discovering love, movies at the Chestnut Hill Theater, and midnight drives through deserted streets and neighborhoods. There were snowstorms: sleeping late in the bed with the heavy blue quilt— warm and quiet underneath. Driving by the exterior of my childhood home in Newton, we reenacted the wonder of memory's intimate spaces; we stopped for ice cream at the White Mountain Creamery on Commonwealth Avenue— the place my brother and I would always reach on our bikes, down the other side of the hill on densely humid summer afternoons. There were the hours of exploring together in Harvard Square, through the musty wonder of used bookstores, the fresh aroma of crisp new volumes in the university shop—to our frequent haunt of the remainder sections at the New England Mobile Bookfair on Needham Street. There we would go for long hours—Leah in the history section, but then making her way with far more delight to the array of cookbooks on sale: her real place of pleasure.

And for all the elaborate cookbooks that filled our kitchen, she never really followed a recipe. Her "problem with authority," she said—but it was actually her intuition as a chef that was the real reason. To the wonder of friends and family, all she needed was a picture of the dish, and then she could make it (and with some added twist you would never think of).

"You do realize how lucky you are to be eating like this, don't you?" one close friend would tease me. I think of that naturalness now—the ease with which she created sensational new dishes, the way she just knew how much of this or that to put in, how to sear the food to its pitch of flavor. I think of how our homes together were always filled with the pleasures and mysteries of scent, bringing guests into our intimate spaces.

That was the way it would be in LA only a few years later, within a month of our arrival on the West Coast. The scene that our friend Adam conjured up in his eulogy at Leah's funeral.

Friends laughing and singing together at the dining room table. Leah emerging from the kitchen with some extraordinary creation of tastes. The voices of little children playing their games of invention and imagination in the next room.

Perfection.

And the refreshing air of California nights gliding through the open screen door.

Abundant platters of chicken with sautéed mushrooms and tomatoes, broccoli florets crisply seared in that rich extra virgin olive oil she loved to use, roasted yams, and the salad made of black beans, corn, tomatoes, and onions. Chilled water on the table, the Shabbat candles glowing on the wooden mantle. A melody slow and deep. First low—contemplative, and from the inner breath—then quickening, as voices merged, the rhythmic drumming of hands on the table. *Nigun* calling out from the depths, *min ha-ma'amakim*. Breath, sound, and speech. Friendship and the wailing of souls, everything at once centered in the moment of meditative song—taking us higher, bringing us deeper into the mystery of Shabbat.

∽

In the stream of memory I am back at Kent Street in Brookline—our first apartment. I remember how we still cooked together then, the old hand-me-down pieces of furniture that composed our living room. Nights going to that vegetarian restaurant on Harvard Street where it was always the tofu soup with cilantro and shitake mushrooms. On Shabbat there were long walks in the park in the afternoon—through streets lined with houses we could only dream of, then on the paths of the Longwood Riverway. Our time of withdrawal and hibernation: just us two in the miraculous space of home.

There were day trips into the country: to Sudbury and Wayland, Lexington and Concord. *I remember how you loved Wilson Farms—overflowing buckets of tomatoes and corn, Red Delicious apples, green seedless grapes, and large pumpkins when they were in season.* Apple cider drawn from the tall cool of refrigerators, and the lines of lush growing plants and flowers running along the pathways and into the garden nursery: azalea, rose, tulip, and iris—a sublime thicket in shafts of sunlight. From there we would return home with our bags full of the season's ripe goodness: strawberries, blueberries, watermelon, and raspberries.

And just as vividly I can see us together in Jerusalem: it was our second year of graduate course work, Leah in modern Jewish history, me in Jewish mysticism and thought. We had a sun-filled little apartment on Klein Street in the heart of Jerusalem's "German Colony," named for the nineteenth-century Europeans who first built up the area. Each day we would travel up the hill, through downtown Jerusalem, to the Hebrew University on Mount Scopus—each to our classes, to quiet hours of study in the library, to long excursions in the shelves of the university bookstore. We were so inseparable even then: finding each other after class for a walk through the wooded trail near the Humanities Division; through the corridors and cobblestone pathways of the campus, to the café for espresso with steamed milk, to the dairy cafeteria in the Social Sciences wing at lunchtime.

Shopping at the little market on our street, cooking together in the white tiled kitchen on Friday afternoons, the smells of approaching Shabbat in the air of the neighborhood. The sun in descent, a cooler silence finding its way through the streets. From the window on Klein Street I could feel it and see it in the movement of the trees, in the shadows that played along the stone walls. And out into the stillness: cars quiet, afternoon heat dissolved into the sweet air of desert night, the Shabbat siren now filling the space.

There were the evenings we ate at Caffit on Emek Refaim—the French onion soup I remember, the pasta with a tomato cream sauce. Outside on the patio we would sit at a table near the street—the cool air of Jerusalem nights warmed by kerosene flame stations. The loneliness of my single days in college had been obliterated by the intimacy of our unspoken language, hands held across the table. We were planning for our future then—every little detail of what was to come. And we were discovering new friendships then—some with couples who now have children, some who split years ago. But it is Friday evenings all together that I remember best—walking back from shul through the

Jerusalem neighborhoods of Rehavia and Baka, down the steep hill by the Jerusalem Theater, past low buildings made of Jerusalem stone.

In the apartment on Klein Street I remember us listening to Sinatra and Dylan as we boiled water for that raspberry-grapefruit infusion tea, or it was Harry Connick Jr. and New Orleans jazz piano while we slowly washed the dishes from dinner: sounds that always brought her back to distant regions of the past and long-forgotten memories.

I can still hear it now as I heard it then: our place of togetherness.

Before we were engaged to be married you asked yourself: if all of my faults could never be fixed, could you accept me as I was? Could I accept you as you were?

In the full realization of love we come to acceptance of imperfection. And maybe those are the deepest secrets we shared—what each of us feared the most, what triggered insecurity in her or me, what made us feel weak or without hope.

I always said that no one could really know me. My core had to remain somehow beyond access, beyond knowing. Though that was before real love. Here in the dark space of emptiness, and after all this time, I realize the extent to which our insides had become one—the measure of our souls blended.

To love deeply. To love in and through imperfection.
To know and to be known.
Standing in and effaced by the circles of time.

9

Suffering

I can barely recall a time when you did not suffer from headaches—it became part of your daily life and our shared frustration, even when you had learned to disguise your pain to others, to go about your life as if nothing was really wrong.

But I always knew. The way her posture would shift ever so slightly, the way her eyes would dart to the side or up to the ceiling. Or she would whisper to me while we were at dinner with friends, and I would hand her the pills under the table—our secret language of pain and coping. And when the facade was finally withdrawn, I would retrieve the blue ice packs from the freezer; I would massage the top of her neck. Our closer friends came to know this as an unyielding part of Leah's life. So many times that I felt the weight of her suffering and I cursed in frustration that she couldn't just have a life without chronic pain, that we together didn't have to feel the unending block to a yearned-for normalcy.

How could we not have known?
How could the early scans not have shown anything?
Is it really possible that these two episodes were unrelated?

And so we sought out the headache specialists: first in Chicago, with the doctor who never made eye contact, and then in Boston with the memorable Dr. S.—the Dutch neurologist who always wore a bow tie and greeted us with a distinctly European gentility and formality. In the waiting room there was a table with cookies and coffee, Dr. S.'s wife sitting as the receptionist who would welcome us when we entered, who would process our payment when we were finished. Dr. S. would often spend forty-five minutes with us in his office—looking up at Leah and me kindly over his desk (I distinctly remember the model brain that sat on the front of that desk, but mostly I remember his compassion and the authentic *presentness* of his care), writing down detailed notes in a condensed yet elegant handwriting. Going to that place together became a kind of pilgrimage—each time hopeful for some breakthrough in healing, and yet always protecting ourselves with the caution made of so many fruitless attempts.

And after many sessions, his ultimate diagnosis: accumulated severe muscle fatigue from years of insomnia; chronic headaches that were linked to the immensity of exhaustion in her body. Only once she could sleep more deeply would the pains in her head subside somewhat. Medications, physical therapy, massage: whatever it would take to ease the pain.

But is it really possible that this was unrelated?

I think now of the vulnerability of the patient as she places her faith in the discernment of doctors. At what point must we simply trust in their judgment, hope that their skill will bring healing? Can we ever really be certain that they have the right answers, that they have not missed the most important clues? Looking back on it now, I am suspicious of all the "experts" we consulted, and I am sharply aware of the degree to which medicine is an art and not a science. I recall the stories told to me of gravely ill patients who received radically contradictory advice from different medical luminaries. What are we supposed to do with that? How much of this search for healing is utterly relative, and how much of it is objective? And yet we—and our innumerable fellow patients—must remain at the unpredictable whim of that art form, hoping and praying that the specialists we consult can find the right answers in time.

I remember well how this struggle with headaches overtook both of our lives, and especially Leah's—it had become a fixture of our existence, a given in the navigation of advanced graduate studies with a serious physical impediment. How do you read hundreds of pages a week when your head feels like it's about to explode from pain? When I recall how frequently Leah was in pain during those years, it amazes me that she came so far in her work toward the PhD (she had passed all her comprehensive exams and was working on the third chapter of her dissertation when illness overwhelmed her). The hours we spent in the Brandeis University Library—in the Judaica reading room, or in the ultraquiet zones of the bottom level. She would often need to take breaks, wandering about the stacks and hallways—and when she felt better I would find her at the long white table outside the reading room, the rows of book stacks only a few feet away, sunlight passing through the broad windows to her right, ten different volumes spread out over the table's surface. Her eyes fixed on the page—legs crossed and back bent in study: I would watch her for a moment from afar before approaching. The warm sensation of seeing the one I love—harbor from the wind and rain, sweet soul attunement in the wide-open land of an unforgiving world.

Other days she would sit in front of a microfilm reading machine on the library's second level, deciphering the handwriting of some nineteenth-century letter writer, recording pages of notes. We would meet up at the front circulation desk where she would be checking out an array of books on American Jewish history, cramming them into the heavy canvas bag that she would lug around campus on her shoulder. Together we would climb the steps to the Humanities Quadrangle, to the Lown Building that houses the Department of Near Eastern and Judaic Studies—to visit with our advisers, to retrieve our mail. I think of how everyone there must have seen us in those days: so rarely were we apart, the departmental administrators came to expect seeing us together. We were the other's anchor and companion in the ordinary reel of daily life.

After so many years at Brandeis, having continued on from college to graduate school at the same place, coming to campus had become more like going to work for the day—returning as dinnertime approached, maybe stopping at the Star Market on Route 30 to pick up a few ingredients for that night's meal; Commonwealth Avenue to Center Street, Center to Langley Road and home. In that apartment in Newton (a suburb I now admit we selected more out of a vague nostalgia for the lost Newton of my childhood) I would be working on my dissertation—trying to finish fast so that I could find a job and lift us out of the impoverished hand-to-mouth existence of graduate students—and Leah would be reading her work in the other room, until it was time to watch television together on the old couch, to go out to the large air-conditioned magic of the movie theater in Natick, or to retreat into hidden intimacy: *Moonlight in Vermont*—candles in the dark.

But the headaches did get better. Compared to how sick she was in the early years of her suffering, it got a lot better after Aderet was born, and especially during our years in Los Angeles. What was the transformative cause? Was it the hormone shift that allowed her to rest more deeply, or was it the mysterious salve of California? Was this there all along? Were those years just a short reprieve from the pain, from the fall downward that was destined to overtake her? I want to make sense of it; I want to know, to understand, to contemplate what we might have done differently. And then I don't: it doesn't matter anymore. She's gone. My Leah is gone.

∽

I sit by her bedside in the ICU at Hackensack Medical Center—part of me still hanging on to shreds of hope. Maybe their efforts to reduce the pressure and swelling in her brain will be successful. Four to five times the normal amount of pressure was pushing hard. Could anyone actually survive that kind of force inside the skull? They had done an emergency bedside procedure to drain some of the fluid out. A hole drilled into her head. A catheter inserted to test the waves of pressure in the brain. They had her on Diprovan and some other drug whose name escapes me now.

"This is usually done in the OR," the neurosurgeon told me. "But she was in a critical condition."

By that he means they thought she was about to die. Right then and there.

But was she already gone by then?

At what point had your mind receded to the other side of darkness, to that place where life withdraws, and there is only a bottomless quiet?

I had to believe then—and I still must believe now—that she was not truly gone until the final moments of good-bye. I have to believe that somehow Leah heard my last words of love.

My pleading with you not to leave. I'm not ready. I'm not ready to lose you.

The indistinct borderlands between the last hours of life and the onset of death.

And yet there is a clear line. Until then she is here—really just asleep, peacefully unconscious. Until then I am able to hold her warm hands, to watch her torso rise and descend with the influx of air from the respirator. There must be something there. Some glimmer of life, some trace of Leah hidden beneath these shadows of coma? I remember thinking: she will still come out of it; she will still wake up. Is there a difference at that moment between believing and hoping?

They come in to examine her at regular intervals. The nurses monitor the IV meds; the lab technician comes in to draw some blood. And when the doctors come in they lift her eyelids, watching for some sign of brain activity.

Pupils unresponsive. Fixed and dilated. That ominous sign of approaching death.

They continue shining the tiny beams of pocket flashlights onto her eyes—searching those depths for any presence of life, any silent indication of some function deep inside.

Anything? I ask each individual who checks her. *Still unresponsive?*

Of course there's nothing new to report—just the immense blanket of darkness that has descended over Leah's eyes, over her brain. I am consumed with the frustration of having to believe these physicians, to just take their word for it. How can they be so damned sure that there is nothing active deep within, that there is no spark of life concealed by these shrouds of death? Perhaps somewhere inside of her there is some heavily veiled consciousness trying to claw its way out from under the illusion of her irreparable brain damage?

I envision it now as a person who has been buried alive, though seemingly dead—only to awaken to the horror of the narrow coffin and the impenetrable darkness, the insurmountable weight of the soil laid above. Was Leah trying to scream out at us: *For God's sake, I am alive in here! You can't see it with your tried-and-true neurological tests, but I'm still here! Don't give up on me yet!* In one of their final examinations they opened her eyes wide, and it was then that I saw the terrible stare of death—the blank gaze from nothing, into nothing.

Still a part of me wanted to protest. How can we really know the mystery and depth of the mind, of the inner self?! How am I supposed to just trust you that she is "already gone"? I think again of the fragility of the medicinal art. Will there come a time in the evolution of medicine when we know more about the true endurance of the brain? Will we understand then that the brain and its consciousness are recoverable after all? Is it conceivable that the threads of consciousness just lie dormant in the skull like the seventeen-year wait of the cicadas beneath the soil—that one day, contrary to all expectation, her original self will emerge, her consciousness will return?

How many unlikelies of healing have been dismissed until the hour of their reversal? How many diseases have been "incurable" and fatal until the horizons of medicine were breached once again? And so I find myself wondering, perhaps only within the realm of imagined possibilities: Are we giving up too soon? How long will it take for medicine to realize that the brain can truly be recovered and jump-started? And what further tragedy of unrealized life will we know then?

The lack of a heartbeat has a greater finality about it. The pulse of life withdraws, and the body begins to change visibly from a living to a dead form. That is what I would witness less than two days later.

Time of death: 12:20 p.m.

The person filled with life and love is now powerfully absent and removed—the eyes that used to look at me from across the room, over the table at dinner, lying next to me in bed.

Now when I wish I could have all those moments back—
I would leave all the books on my night table unread, *and
it would be only you and your warmth.* The shape of her that I
remember, though the bed forgets; perfect intimacy in the
quiet space of love.

∽

Tuesday, February 27, 2007. 11:35 p.m. I did not know it
then, but less than thirty-seven hours remained until Leah's
heart would beat for the last time.

Time of death: "12:20 p.m. Thursday, March 1." So it reads
on the Death Certificate I now hold in my hands. The offi-
cial stamp and signature of the New Jersey Department of
Health, Bureau of Vital Statistics.

I study the form:

> *Legal name of decedent.*
> *Name of surviving spouse.*
> *Method of disposition.*
> *Immediate Cause.*

Here is the stark record of the end. *The place you take in the
records of the state.*

I wake in the ICU waiting area—I have slept for an
hour or so on the long red couch. Lights and images flicker
on the television screen; the volume has been lowered near
to silence. For a moment I linger in the liminal space of in-
between; I savor the evanescent feeling that none of this is
real. I was dreaming. I was just dreaming.

But it comes back all too soon, and the illusion of dream recedes. The waiting room is empty at this hour—though someone has left some clothes and food on a nearby table. I had wanted to rest in the room with Leah, on the chair next to her bed and IV dispenser, but the ICU nurses told me that they strongly requested family members not sleep in the rooms. If her condition were to crash, they would need to get to her without a sleeping husband in the way. I said I understood, even though leaving her side didn't feel right. And yet I was exhausted. We had been up together, virtually nonstop, since Monday. It had been more than forty hours without rest. And the marathon of almost total sleeplessness would press on through this night and the next.

By the time I am awake and on my feet, I realize that my mother must have arrived already from Chicago. Barbara, Leah's mom, had been with me in the ICU since 7:30 p.m. or so—before that she was at our house, taking care of Aderet, trying to keep things calm. She tells me that she has been cleaning and organizing our house from top to bottom. Her way of dealing with the nervous energy, she says. And now Jack, Leah's dad, is here as well. I can see the brokenness in their eyes already, a shattering of the parent's soul. There would be no redemption—only a prayer for a miracle. A miracle we all knew was not coming.

The neurologist comes by to talk with us. They would be watching Leah closely over these next few hours, through the night and into the morning. If there was to be any improvement, it would need to come in these next couple of days—beyond that, it would be assumed that severe brain damage had occurred, irreparable loss.

So I sit by her bed, her hand clasped tightly in mine, the feel of her wedding ring against my skin. Her mouth is held slightly ajar by the breathing tube, the right side of her scalp shaven for the insertion of the catheter into her skull. Even now I cannot remove that image from my mind—she lies there so still. In the turn of an instant, that which was my normal and my compass has been pulled from me. Would she return?

The silence in the room is deep and complete—only the whisper and hush of the respirator make the rhythm of time, the marker of a new time. Could she hear me? I press my face against hers; I kiss her lips—the side of her mouth untouched by the large plastic tube.

"Lealie," I whisper in her ear.
"I love you."
The rise and fall of the respirator fills the space between
    my words.
"I'm not ready . . . I'm not ready to lose you . . ."

I rub my cheek and my nose along her right arm, familiar freckles, familiar milky skin. I drink in her scent, drawing my face over her. It is Leah's smell, her softness, and her warmth. I rest my head there, trying all the while not to disrupt the delicate wires and IV lines that are connected to her.

From a place deep inside comes the melody of our wedding day—slow and rhythmic, the approach of the bride to the groom. It is a Hasidic melody, filled with a longing rescued from a lost world: with each wave and tone I can see my love walking toward me, concealed in her veil, and yet glowing with the promise of years to come.

My face pressed against her soft arm, I sing it to her again—escorting her again, waiting again for her approach. Entering into that *nigun*, I am swept away beyond the frames of time and space defined by this hospital room; I am back in the warmth and safety of her company—stroking my head, holding my hand. The nurses and other family members can come and go from the room, but I have been lifted beyond it: into the ethereal present of the eternal *you*, into the dream that is the two of us—in our time of living, in our time of forward looking.

The hospital is quiet and empty during the early-morning hours. Only as the shadows wash away under the fresh columns of dawn—otherworldly radiance, luminal birth, and reawakening—only in those movements does the night give way to a new shift, the reemergence of visitors and hospital staff.

My mother brings me a hot cup of coffee from the lobby; she comes back up accompanied by a colleague of mine from the Seminary—a rabbi who is also a family friend. He has driven out from Manhattan to visit us. I do my best to receive him, and we embrace.

"Bill—so sweet of you to come," I say.

"How are you managing?" he asks gently. His eyes are full of compassion.

"I'm . . . trying . . ."

I pause for a long moment. And then: "It's just devastating, really . . . So hard to believe."

My hands take in some of the warmth of the coffee. My legs feel strangely rooted in the ground, and yet there is this odd sensation of floating.

"I feel like it's all so unreal, you know? Yesterday she's up and about, doing okay—the next afternoon, we're here and she's . . . *gone*. It can't be real—*this can't be real*, I keep telling myself. And at the same time it feels like it couldn't be more real . . . I don't know . . . I don't know . . ."

I am quiet; my eyes fall to the ground. I am finding it hard to make eye contact—a state that would continue for many days after Leah's death.

"I don't really know when I'll be able to come back to teaching," I say to him. "My head is just spinning right now."

"Of course," he responds. "Don't even think about that right now. There is nothing more important than what you are going through."

10

Where Are You? What Endures?

Now, at the close of Passover: not even five weeks out. The heartache washes over me, and I am in its inescapable grip. My breathing becomes both heavy and shallow, my chest filled with the sorrow of sinking. When it fills me I am pulled into a forest of darkness—the black hole of dissolving futures. I try again to breathe. In through my nose, long exhalation through pursed lips. But it is not quite the same as stress. It is a more unconquerable ache. Heartache. Soul-ache. A hollow ache at the center of my body. My stomach feels it too, and my throat and my legs. How is it that someone can burrow down so deep inside as to dwell in your very bones, to inhabit the pathways of your circulation? A presence so thorough that its withdrawal feels like a dying in my own self, a death inside of me?

Your wife died, but you did not die—so I read in one of the books
   on my night table.
You did not die.
But am I living?

We lit a memorial candle for Leah this Passover holiday—aglow next to the remembrances of other lives. Incandescence of memory, slow-burning marker of a soul-spark.

And what endures? A presence?

My mother said she had the strangest sense of your presence watching over her as she played with Aderet on her bedroom floor.

What remains?

The traces of her handwriting, scattered through the house? What of her body that lies concealed by earth? Does that which was Leah return to an undifferentiated continuum of Being? Is it truly *dust to dust*—elements recalled to their most basic roots in the fabric of the world? I think of what Aderet asks about the time before she was born, before she was even conceived and carried in Imma's tummy.

Was I in the stars then, Abba? she asks.

In the stars. Absorbed in the elements of nature, contained in the shimmer of distant lights.
But alive. Living before, and living after.

To imagine a state of nonexistence, a time when there was no *me*, is instinctively difficult, even impossible. And to imagine the space of death is just the same—to have crossed the boundaries of what we know as real, an inability to accept that what we know as *living* ever morphs into something else. *Not living? Dead?* What is that? I can't fathom it—how could I ever expect a four-year-old child to grasp it?

I read the calming advice of Thich Nhat Hanh, paraphrasing the wisdom of the Buddha: in this world we are but manifestations, disclosures of the always enduring continuum of Life. To die is to withdraw from manifestation; it is not to cease to be.

In the stars.

Is that too the ethereal house of your presence?

The same stars we would count on Saturday nights at the close of Shabbat—the three of us standing in the backyard of our home in Los Angeles, lights of another world peering down at us in our earth-time. And I think of how those lights are but the remnants of a place in the galaxy now long gone, burned up in the expanse of time it has taken to reach our perception down here. So do they live? Or are they but the traces of what once was?

To Aderet I read Tomie de Paola's classic story *Nana Upstairs, Nana Downstairs*—his gentle narration of death, of love and loss in a child's world. I remember the magic of this story from my own childhood: a shooting star as the kiss of memory, the flash of transcendent presence. She kisses you good night from that luminous place, from the great Beyond in the brilliant vault of heaven. She is there—radiant and in motion in the night sky.

Read it again, Abba, she says.

Read the dying part again.

ა

I have not yet been back to the grave since your burial.

Will I feel your presence there?

In the Jewish mystical tradition it is believed that a portion of the soul remains in and around the grave—a sacred trace of the life we knew in this world. *But are you really there?* Like Aderet, I just can't bring myself to imagine that Leah's *entirety* has been erased. Even to think of her as absorbed back into the womb of existence, swallowed into the stream of oneness, is unacceptable to me. *Something of your individual self, your you-ness, must remain!* And it can't be that she only remains intact in my memories, only in the memories of Aderet, those of parents, parents-in-law, grandparents, of sister and brother. That's all just pitiful consolation. Something I would have said with sincerity to someone else before I experienced it myself.

I wonder if I can pinpoint the moment when Leah's spirit began to depart, when the person who lived this life was no longer, and all that remained was the physical shell. It's just so difficult to talk about her, think about her, in any way that is removed from that physical presence. How can I separate her spirit or soul from the familiar voice, from the touch of her skin, from the scent of her hair and face? The way she crossed her legs or pointed her toes; the way she scratched her ears or rubbed her eyes. The way she would sit on the couch, her feet lifted up—the soft tan blanket draped over her legs; the way she would climb the stairs in our house or flip a stir-fry with a quick motion of her wrist. The way she would sit in the bath and let the running water pour over her head and neck. She calls to me, and I wrap a warm towel around her—she looks at me with the face of love.

All the little physical details are so much more real to me than any spirit or soul could ever be. It is the great irony of our resistance to mortality—our pushing back against the finality and haunting emptiness of death. We cling to this notion of an enduring soul, of a spirit that lives on, though dislodged from its physical chamber.

But I want to scream out against it.

It's your living body that I want! Gone to your eternal rest in the heavenly Garden of Eden? To hell with that—I want you here!

Departed spirit. The persistence of life beyond death.

Or is it the massive emptiness of nothingness—the weightless evaporation into complete nonexistence?

Where are you now? Are you at all?

But Aderet and I do still talk to Leah each night as our final bedtime ritual—a deep testimony, I suppose, to a stubborn belief that some measure of a life transcends death. I encourage Aderet to tell her mom about the day she has had—what little things we did that would make Imma smile, that would make her proud. Tonight she tells me that Imma can't really hear what we are saying (her own awareness of death's elusiveness), and to my surprise I find myself insisting that she can.

She can hear us. We really are speaking to her. Even in death she is somehow alive, reachable.

I realize that despite my disbelief, there is something powerfully true in that. Something immediate and real. As we talk out loud to Leah ("Guess what I did today, Imma!"), I feel a lightness filling my heart and throat—as though my suspension of disbelief takes me into the embrace of an alternate universe, a place where time has been suspended in the days before tragedy struck. Aderet smiles and talks with love to her mom. Things are good again, safe again— if only for a short while.

11

Snowfall

It is the middle of April now, but the snow is falling here in Chicago, at my parents' home. Sitting in my father's study, at his desk, I watch the flood of snowflakes sweeping through the air. We came here as planned for the second half of the Passover holiday (and I survived the much-dreaded solo-parent trip through the airports—eyes in the back of my head, a pink princess bag stuffed full with snacks and games to keep a four-year-old entertained, a change of her clothes, and more, and more), but I decided to extend our stay for another five days. A short reprieve from the reality of our inevitable return to the empty house in New Jersey—a little relief from having to be the only one looking after Aderet, keeping her happy, keeping her safe.

Such a strange snowfall. Seems so out of place at this point in the cycle of seasons. Hadn't we already passed into spring? When the sun had finally warmed things up, after shivah was over, I thought it was such a shame that Leah missed the rising of spring from this cold winter—she would have loved to see that, our first spring in the new house. Soon she would have wanted to put the rocker in the entry room with all the windows and the light.

You would have had a blanket with you, and a cup of tea. You would be reading, and Aderet would play on the floor beside you.

Sun washing through the windowpanes—Leah's little space in the world, her small corner of delight.

12

My Child's Voice

You are my sunshine, my only sunshine, you make me happy when skies are gray. . . . Please don't take my sunshine away.

The song plays on the car stereo, and I know that something is on Aderet's mind. Looking out the window, she is quiet; she is sucking her thumb. And so I ask her.

"I'm thinking about Imma, Abba. Because Imma used to sing this song to me when she was alive."

My child's simple words have the power to bring me back into the moment—again the emotions are raw, the sorrow is deep. When the track has finished, she asks me to repeat it—over and over again. And I comply: "You Are My Sunshine" becomes a kind of returning elegy— the refrain of a little girl's longing, the pulse of a father's helplessness.

"I want my Imma. When I see the green tree I think of Imma, and when I see the sunshine I think of Imma and how she sang 'You Are My Sunshine' to me."

∽

During the day we sit together, recording the feelings and the memories. I write them down in the pocket notebook I now carry—for those frequent moments when the impulse to write comes over me unexpectedly. And out of

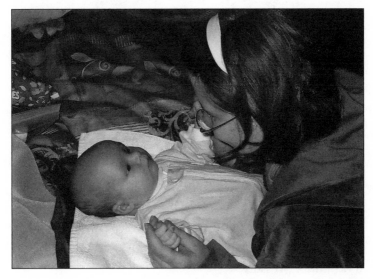

You're my Imma!

her pours a confession, a child's reverie—her own song of
longing and mourning:

> *I miss my Imma, and I miss playing with my Imma.*
> *I liked getting hugged from my Imma and Abba.*
> *So nice. Love, Aderet.*
>
> *I want to play a game with Imma.*
> *I only want to play a game with you, Imma—*
> *you're the only one who I want to play the game with.*
> *I love you.*
> *Thank you for being my Imma.*
> *I love you. I miss you.*
> *I remember giving hugs to Imma—*
> *I remember when my Imma gave me hugs and kisses.*

I want you, Imma.
Please let her be here.
I want you a bushel and a peck and a hug around the neck.
I want you.

I want Imma. I miss her.
I feel so sad.
I cannot wait to see her again.

I realize that, like me, she too needs to share what she's feeling. We grievers are possessed with the intense desire and need to speak about our loss and our pain: to release that which is otherwise bottled up in the heart like contents under pressure.

Abba, I love my Imma. I miss her.
I remember when my Imma used to read me princess books.
Sleeping Beauty, Cinderella, Snow White, Belle.

Imma got my blankie warm for me,
and I can't wait to see her again.
I also said that last time, but I wanted to say it two times.

I love when my Imma used to snuggle with me.
With my blankie and me.
You know what? She always used to want my blankie when
*   she was being silly.*
She would say: "I want my blankie!"
Abba, I miss my Imma.

Imma, I want you too and I love you too.
Then I'll give you a big hug.
I love you even bigger than the world.

I miss you. I love you.

I will hug you when you come back.
I can't wait to see you again.

Love, Aderet.

I loved it when she would read me stories
and bring me snacks every day.

I want her, I want her.

I wonder when she's coming back,
I want to see her here,
I want to, want to see her,
I only want to see her.

You are my sunshine, my only sunshine,
you make me happy when skies are gray,
you'll never know dear how much I love you,
please don't take my sunshine away.
Good-night, I love you,
I love you, I love you.
You love me too.

I will paint you in different colors.
I love you pink, I love you yellow and white,
I love you even in green and all the way
from my toes to my head.
You are my sunshine, you are my sunshine . . .
Please don't take my sunshine away . . .
Imma, I can't wait to see you again!
I want you to try to see me again around the world.

Aderet on Leah's shoulders

I love you, one,
I love you, two,
I love you, three . . .

That's the end of my Imma song.
Fishbane family, good night.
Imma, good night.

∽

I have been postponing the task of going through the papers on Leah's desk and shelves, but I still find myself drawn to the room where they lie—traces of her living presence, markers of her mind at work. There are folders filled with typed and handwritten notes for the chapter of her dissertation she was working on, little fragments of which I remember her trying to tell me about.

But alongside the archival lists and the folders of unfinished work, beside the shelves of books on modern Jewish history, there are the memory books that Leah constructed: pictures and bits of our family's material history. The first picture taken of Aderet as a sonogram when she still lived in Leah's womb; the pink hospital ID bracelet, mother and daughter with matching numbers; the imprint taken of Aderet's feet by the nurses. And all of these placed by Leah in a large album with a rough ivory cover, set aside for a quiet future moment when we would reminisce together about the time we became a family of three. Now these are the talismans of memory—the fragments of an amazing grace that serve as pathways in my mind, corridors to the big rooms of the past. And these fragments that I hold in my hand, they bring the past forward to me—both as knife to the wound and as the healing herb of some primal medicine.

In her study, the library books I retrieved for her are speckled with little note cards and Post-Its. Thoughts she was planning to come back to? A citation she was planning to use in a new chapter? I see the scattered fruit of all those long hours in the Philadelphia archives, the summer when I stayed home with fifteen-month-old Aderet in our little rented apartment, while Leah spent her days poring over archival documents. It was a time of powerful bonding for us, father and daughter.

I think back to that time now as I struggle to get my bearings as a single father (*single*—still such a strange status to find myself in after all these years), as I learn to do ordinary things that were always Leah's province. Packing lunch for school and getting Aderet dressed (a drama with unending variation for a little girl so excited by the assembly of matching outfits and princess colors!). The hours before bed: the procession of bath, pajamas, and the brushing of teeth. And then there is the series of requests, called out from bed in her adorable, high-pitched little voice; the sequence of bad dreams in which I sit beside her on her bed, stroking her hair and her shoulders. I am the only one there to answer her now. There are no more turns to be taken.

In the morning she has something urgent to tell me:

Abba, I ripped a napkin in the kitchen. Do you know why? Because that makes me feel sad about Imma.

Is this her way of reenacting what she saw me do during the first week of mourning? The rip in my shirt just over the left side of my chest? I think of the moment of Leah's death in the hospital, when, as is the custom, we each ripped a piece of our clothing. Wordless testimony to our bearing witness: the passage from life to death.

Aderet tells me that she wants to go see Imma at the cemetery. She saw "Imma's bed" (what she called Leah's covered casket at the funeral home), but wants to see where we "hid" Imma.

I pause for a moment.

"Do you understand what happens at the cemetery?" I ask. "Do you know where Imma is?"

"Yes," she says—"she's under the ground!"

I don't remember really explaining this to her; if I did, I certainly didn't expect her to understand it.

I see from her face that she is very eager to go, to have something concrete to associate with "Imma's bed." I think of the tender way Leah's sister, Stephanie, recalled to me our act of shoveling soil into Leah's open grave. We were tucking her in. Pulling the covers up nice and tight.

Fishbane family, good night.
Imma, good night.

Am I projecting a fear of graves onto her? We talk about visiting the earth where Leah is buried; we talk about bringing flowers for Imma and a special note for Imma too. "I want to do that," Aderet says. "I want to put flowers on Imma's bed."

We are up again much of the night—Aderet calls to me every ten minutes from her bedroom. She is plagued by bad dreams—the on-and-off crying lasts from 3:00 to 5:00 a.m. At a certain point I feel like I am losing my mind—a tumult of sleeplessness and frustration—in and out of bed without rest. Here is the life of a single parent. My partner is gone. And my child's grief surfaces in these dreadful midnight moments—together we are adrift.

Eventually she falls asleep. We both wake late—the overcast clouds of exhaustion and sadness looming for the day that is to come.

∽

A Sunday morning—spring is now in full bloom, the warm air cleaning out the last of winter's cold shadow. Aderet wants to read the book of drawings that her little classmates made for her in the days following Leah's death. Such pure expressions of consolation: a child's intuition of grieving and the pain of loss. Filled with multicolored works of child art, the messages dictated to the teacher-scribes read:

> *I want to make you feel better.*
> *I hope you don't cry.*
> *Here is a picture of your family.*

I read the message from her friend Russell:

> *Your Imma still loves you.*

And Aderet says: "I like that one the best 'cause he says my Imma still loves me."

I think of the line from the Song of Songs: "Love is strong as death." Will death yield to the love of a four-year-old child for her mother? In the greatness of our love we seek to press beyond those rigid borders, beyond that dreaded darkness of finality, of ultimate loneliness.

Aderet sits on my lap. We are reading the story *Beauty and the Beast*. She interrupts and says: "I love my Imma. I miss her too much."

"I know, baby. What made you think of Imma just now?"

"Well, we were reading *Beauty and the Beast* and Gaston died. And that made me think of Imma. Abba, I want to visit Imma in the hospital."

"Sweetie, Imma's not in the hospital anymore."

"But I want to see her there. I want to see her in her death. When I die and when you die we'll all be smushed together again, right? Abba, can Imma eat when she's not alive?"

The directness of her question takes me aback for a moment.

"No, sweetheart—she can't."

She protests. "But Abba, if she can't eat she'll get sick again!"

I see that she too, like her father, is still trying to protect her mom.

∽

She wakes wailing and crying. It takes me a while to realize what she is saying, but gradually it becomes clear. She is crying out for her Imma:

I want you . . . I want you . . .

I come into her bedroom. She is so tired that she has already fallen back asleep, but when I go to fix her covers she wakes for a moment.

"Did you see Imma in your dream?" I ask her.

She nods. Her thumb in her mouth, her voice soft and sad.

"What happened in your dream?"

"Imma was falling off a cliff! She was falling and falling to her death!"

My God.

I shake inside for my baby girl. Powerless to stop her falling mother. The terrifying sensation of dream-fall becomes the slipping away of her protection, the center of her world. I could hear the terror and the fear in her first screams. That was it. Dead. Gone.

In the morning I ask her again about her dream; I need to know that she is okay. In the meantime she has added a new element to the story:

> She was falling almost to her death, but I flew like Tinkerbell, and I caught her and she was in my arms, and I gave her some pixie dust and she flied with me! I was almost to death, but I gave her pixie dust and brought her up to the top. And then she never fell. I was being safe with her.
>
> Abba, can our dreams ever come true? 'Cause I wanted to save her for real. I wanted to save her for real, Abba.

She never fell. For real. I wanted to save her for real! In this moment I am desperate for the magic of her Disney-inspired belief. Can I too be absorbed into a world where believing in magic is enough to make magic happen? Is there a plane of being in which the dream of redemption can dissolve the clamp of nightmare?

As I watch her, I realize that the artwork she makes for Leah is her instinctive form of grief therapy. Like my own need to write, Aderet needs to channel her pain and bewilderment into creativity as well. Without saying a word to me, she takes out the implements of drawing (paper, markers, stickers—all of which were ordered by Leah, and carefully placed in the family room drawers), and she begins her work.

"Abba, this sticker is Imma, this sticker is you, this one is me." Then she begins to sing. Another elegy, another melody of longing:

Good night, my Imma, I love you—
I want you for the night,
I can't sleep without you.
I can't have a world without you—
I want you to see me now,
I can't wait to see you again.
And I can't even wait until you come back,
let me now know that you're here—
I won't do anything until you are back.

Love, Aderet.

On the couch downstairs she clutches a white blanket to her chest; she pulls it up close to her face.

"Imma used to lie with this blankie," she says. "It still smells like Imma, so I like to hold it and I like to smell it."

She slides herself off the couch—thumb in her mouth, blanket held tight. Then from the shelf she retrieves the special purple box we have designated as "Imma's box"—inside she keeps all the little items that connect her to Leah.

"You see this mirror, Abba? If you look in it, you can see Imma!"

"Oh, that's terrific!" I say. "Just like the mirror that the Beast gives to Belle when she leaves the castle! So she can always find her way back to him."

"Yeah, that's right! And in this one, I can see my Imma!"

"What's she doing in the mirror? What do you see in there?"

"Well, I see her cooking dinner! She's making pizza and other things. Oooh! And here's an Imma bear! If you cuddle with this bear, you'll feel Imma softing your back. And here's a magic bracelet! If you wear this bracelet, you'll feel Imma stroking your *keppie*."

"What are these?" I ask, holding two small drawings between my fingers.

"Abba, those are pictures that Imma made of me, and if you hold these pictures to your ears, you'll hear Imma saying, *I love you, Aderet*."

"Oh, sweetheart, that's so beautiful. Imma will always love you, and she will always watch over you." I hold her close; I kiss her cheek for a long moment.

These objects are the memories that can be held in hand; they are charged with the magic of a child's pure hope. To transcend the heartbreak and the absence—to find her way back to innocence through the magic mirror and this wondrous box of dreams.

She asks me to turn on the voice recorder that I have bought, and she begins to sing again:

I loved it when Imma would take care of me,
she would take good care of me.
Please don't take her away,
no, don't take her away!
I want her back,
I love her,
please don't ever say I don't love her.

Please don't say she's not my mommy,
please always let her be my mommy.

I'm sad because she died.
I liked playing princess games with her.
I love you, I love you,
please come with me!
Please give her back to me!
I love her so much . . .

13

Spaces in Memory

I am relatively okay for large stretches of time. I think part of my old self has returned. Then, with the force and suddenness of a slamming door, I am back in the throes of it— the hollow, sinking ache. My first impulse is to call Leah. To pick up the phone, or to walk in the front door ready to unburden myself into her presence. To enter back into the space of home.

The places we inhabit end up shaping our imaginations, our dreams and reveries of what was in our past, of what secrets lie concealed within drawers and closet doors. The dining room—transfigured through the festive meals of Shabbat, when the changed contours of time remade the ordinary into the sacred. The couch where she would sit, the kitchen where she would cook, the backyard where she would play on summer days with Aderet. We re-create the world through the naming of spaces as chambers for our things and our daily routines; they become the vessels of memory's formulation. Houses whose interiors were markers of intimacy and hope, the new house that was the realized dream of togetherness, suddenly becomes the interior of solitude, the marker of our future's deconstruction and banishment.

It is the emptiness of the bedroom closet and the drawers; the spaces where her things were neatly and casually placed, ready to be recovered and drawn out for one occasion or another, ready for her to wear, just as she left them. Upon returning from out of town, I discovered that our well-meaning housecleaners had gone through these drawers and removed all of Leah's clothing: all re-placed in organized bags in the next room. I remember feeling overwhelmed with the desire to riffle through the bags and put the items back in their rightful places. Her things needed to remain in the drawers; they needed to hang as they were in the closet!

I feel Leah's living presence in the softness of her remaining clothes. When I finally found her blue checkered pajamas, I remember feeling an immense relief—I could still hold those bits of clothing to my chest at night. I suddenly understand the power of Aderet's desperation when she cannot locate her special pink blankie. Holding it close takes the edge off the fright of loneliness and the terrors of darkness.

The physical space of emptiness and quiet seems to parallel the rhythms of my interior space, the chambers of my own head. I want to ask her advice on some small (or large) matter; I am not used to making decisions by myself. There was nothing—not even the most trivial of things—that we didn't process together, obsess over together. And so quickly, the interior space of my mind—an extension of my unending talk with Leah—is left in bewildering solitude. I am left with the words unspoken in my head, wanting desperately to articulate them, to confess them to her.

∽

I haven't been back to the city and to Seminary Row in almost two months now. Part of me can't bear the thought of pulling out of the parking garage, turning left onto 122nd, and crossing Broadway toward Riverside Drive. *Because that's when I would always call to tell you that I was on my way home for dinner.* Home, interior spaces: the four walls of memory and intimacy. On winter nights when I would close my car door and approach the house, I could often smell the fire Leah had started—curled up in her favorite spot, soaking in the soul-restoring heat of a home fire. Smoke moving well out through the chimney and into the night air, the perfect intersection of the aromas of home—fireplace, dinner, family. Opening the front door, and hearing: "Hi, Abba! . . . Hi, Eitee!"

As I recite the kaddish, these are the images that float inside of me. Driving home from a day of teaching in Los Angeles at Hebrew Union College, stepping onto the driveway to hear the sweet sounds of play in the backyard, where Leah was engaged in some wonderful bit of imagination with Aderet—sidewalk chalk coloring, painting at the easel, watering the garden. Or if the sun had set already, I would come close to the side door and listen furtively to them in the kitchen—preparing dinner together, waiting for me to come home. The sounds of love, the sounds of family—the deep tones of memory.

14

Photographs

In the days following Leah's death, amid the flurry of visitors and the week of shivah, I would retreat to my study on the third floor, seeking some respite from the seemingly endless stream of well-wishers and consolers. Not that I didn't appreciate their coming, or that I didn't derive some comfort from knowing that they were there. I did. But after a while of sitting with them in the living room, recounting the story of Leah's sudden illness and death again and again, I would take a little time for myself in the private spaces of the second and third floors—my public grief located downstairs, the private secluded above.

And it was in those hours of withdrawal that I began compiling the photographs—the visual record of our passage from a couple into a family. The countless pictures that Leah took—images of Aderet in scores of different poses and moments. But each surviving image of Leah is now a treasure to me, never to be recaptured.

So many of them were taken during our family trip up the California coast in June 2005—when we set out north on the Pacific Coast Highway, the legendary road simply known as "the 1" or "the PCH" to Southern Californians. We picked up the PCH in Santa Monica, speeding past Wilshire and Sunset boulevards, through the overlying hills and ocean-blue expanse of the Pacific Palisades and Malibu. Fruit stands, farm fields, and beaches as we made our way in and out of Oxnard, Ventura, and then Santa Barbara. Our goal was to reach San Luis Obispo by midafternoon, to use that central coast location as a base from which we might explore the surrounding area—textures of brilliance, fields of wine waiting to be made.

I linger over the photographs that remain from that space in my memory, and each one opens up an avenue to images I would have otherwise forgotten—tunnels in the dark that surface back into the blinding light of vivid images. There are the pictures from one of our highlights: fruit picking at Avila Valley Farm, from which we returned to LA with cartons full of freshly plucked raspberries and oallaberries; memories of our meandering through the farm store, selecting one or another jar of farm-made jam. There are the pictures of Leah holding Aderet close as the awakening winds of the central coast power through their hair and clothes. In front of the ripe green rows of vineyard crop (the heart of California wine country), or beside the mind-blowing bluffs near San Simeon: crystal, sparkling tides, the jagged edges of the coast rock bespeaking the rough force and wildly luminous soul of that sea current. When we stopped for a picture, and to take in the majesty, we knew we were in the presence of something mighty and mysterious. The gusts of wind enough to knock you over, but if you stand firm—heart turned open to receive the lust of nature's desire—you will feel it fill your body with the hunger and completion of a lover's embrace, the infusion of breeze rippling through you like a mixing of divine wines in your soul.

Leah and Aderet picking berries at Avila Valley Farm

And onward up the coastal road, where the dream-
land open space yields to the labyrinthine pathways of Big
Sur—a texture of green and a cloud-laced mountain wonder, an ascent into a mystery that feels like a hermitage
secluded from the ravages of time. Or it was Cambria, the
small town set deep into an off-coast valley where we col-
lected multicolored scent at a spice and aroma store. And
these are still locked into a small glass bottle that Leah
procured, a vial of memory that we resurrect as late Saturday afternoon crosses the threshold from the Sabbath day
to the eve of the new week.

There they are.
Leah and Aderet playing in the backyard in LA: the
happiness on my wife's face is deep and full; her joy in

being present to Aderet, the calm in feeling so absorbed in a community of friends. Leah came into her own in that place—children playing together on the sidewalk and on the green lawns of Shabbat afternoons, sitting with friends on our back patio as the wind chime was lifted into dance and song.

There's the photograph of us just before we went out dancing. It was our anniversary.

I remember how happy she was that night, and how beautiful. It was the Derby in Silver Lake—a place that preserves the mood and burgundy glamour of old Hollywood. We sat in one of the oversized crescent booths near the bar and the front dance floor: dinner, dessert, and the simple pleasure of held hands; slow-burning candles and big-band music.

Another image takes me to the playground in Montauk, New York—at the outermost point of Long Island. Leah and Aderet are seated side by side on the swing set—Leah dressed in her soft black knits, her posture and her expression just as I remember them. I can still feel the air as the three of us walked down the sand-and-gravel path to the water—the large rocks strewn across the wild and untamed roughness of the shoreline; the lighthouse looming high above. Something protected and sacred in that moment: withdrawn from the towns and the cities, secluded in our own intimacy, our own circle of speech. This was family: mother, father, and daughter.

At long last I find the courage to watch the videotapes that we had recorded, knowing I would encounter the realness of her voice, the apparition of her living movements.

Leah and Aderet reading

And as I enter into the sweet space of Aderet's second birthday party (how amazing now to recall Aderet's voice and speech from that stage of development—I had forgotten how much change there has been in just two years, how she speaks now like an articulate little girl!), I am overcome with Leah's familiar sound, expressions, gestures. I can feel the welling up of a deep sadness that had hidden itself for a short while; the sting of bittersweetness is sharp and immediate.

Her voice surfaces to me as though from the depths of a lost world; the past like an infinite mystery opens its mouth to the present, a primordial wind over the face of the deep. And her voice, her sound—they summon Leah to life again, even if only within the echoing rooms of my mind.

There she is; and there she is not: captured in the merging illusions of dream, remembrance, and the trick of digital images.

This is the housing of memory: the chambers of long cultivation, the concealment beneath the soil of a gardener's winter, the season of its reemergence and the flowering of new life. I am filled with an overpowering desire to have her back, for my life to be restored to the way it was. Against all my knowledge of the way the world works, against every rational thought in my head, I still find myself hoping for this to somehow magically transpire. She will come back to me; she will come back to her baby and her family—from across the chasm of distance and all mortality.

15

Motherless

As I unbuckle her from her car seat, Aderet asks me: "Can daddies get so sick and die too?"

I recognize in her the same insecurity and fear of death that I am feeling. Perhaps she thinks: Will this cruel world leave me even more abandoned, even more alone? How can I really know that I am safe when the person who was my safety has been taken away? For all of my unconditional love for her, for all of my attempts to be mother and father rolled up in one, I cannot really do that.

You're Imma and Abba now, she says. *Is Imma inside of you, Abba?*

And I feel myself somehow channeling fragments of Leah's personality and presence in my play with Aderet. A gesture, an expression, a way of speaking: all of a sudden both of us will recognize it as Imma's—and then I wonder (Aderet wonders too) if some trace of Leah's self has remained alive inside of me, awakened in unexpected moments, allowing me to serve as the physical vessel for a now otherworldly spirit.

But there is just a fundamental difference between a man and a woman: something unique and irreplaceable about a mother's love. Is it a purity of love? I think of Leah's seemingly endless patience and creativity in caring for

Aderet, in discovering new ways to bring out our child's learning and character.

Will she grow up so scarred by this state of being motherless that she will never be able to fully trust another person? Will she feel loved enough by me to face the harsh road of this world? And what of her maturation from the little pumpkin she is now into a young woman finding her way through the thorny emotions of adolescence and growing up? Will I be able to teach her those things? What do I really know about being a girl, about coming of age as a woman? They say that a daughter never fully recovers from the absence of a mother's love, and despite our attempts to talk to Leah at bedtime, her living voice is so profoundly missing. Can I even begin to fill that void, that cavern of darkness? Will I fail her? *Will I fail?*

Several friends have remarked to me about the uncanny resemblance they see between Aderet and her mom. Leah used to refer to it as Aderet's "eye smile"—the way each eye creases noticeably on its outer edge when she smiles. It is her mouth-smile too, and the delicious little dimple on her cheek. The way her hair falls by the nape of her neck, the way it curls up in wisps and waves. Now it is one of the many physical markers that Leah has left behind in Aderet. Her little child's glasses, and the shape of her face when she gets excited and silly. When she was first born, everyone commented on the striking resemblance between Aderet and me—she was the spitting image of her father, especially when compared to my baby pictures.

So Leah would joke:

Hello, some of us had to go through labor! Don't you think
she looks just a little like me?

But I read somewhere that the father-baby resemblance is
nature's way of encouraging a bond with the dad when
the baby so instinctively cries for her mother's touch, her
mother's voice. Barbara and Jack tell me that Aderet's personality is just like Leah's was at this age: precocious and
full of bubbly energy. Full of life. I wonder how my baby
girl will carry that legacy into the years ahead. What will
the traces be, both visible and hidden—what markers
of Leah's life will be revealed through our daughter? If I
can bring myself to believe in immortality, then that is it.
Beyond all death, she will live in Aderet—in the girl and
woman she is destined to become.

Aderet tells me that when she is a mommy, she will
wear Imma's glasses (they sit now on my bureau as a haunting reminder), and when she is a mommy she will read the
books in Imma's study. She says that she will also write a
chapter, just the way Imma did. She will be Leah's spirit-
breath in the world of the living—her continuation, her
new incarnation.

16

Interlude of Memory

Late October, 1999. The day after our wedding (raucous joy, entranced shimmer of cloud-flight, sweet contentment), we set out for West Townshend, Vermont, and the fire-lit enchantment of Windham Hill Inn. From northern Westchester it took us the afternoon and into the evening (including our partially anticipated losing of the way), and we arrived for our first dinner at the inn not earlier than 9 p.m. But they had our table waiting for us—near the fireplace, enveloping tones of burgundy and washed white.

It was a big converted house—white with a brick exterior—but they had transformed and renovated the old barn into a new detached section of the inn, just a bit more secluded than the main house. The large room with an antique four-post wooden bed frame, the fireplace where we sat together, listening to one of the meditative collections of acoustic guitar instrumentals; the broad windowpanes looking out on the green expanse of farmland. Walking the path from the barn to the main house for dinner, I remember us breathing in crisp mountain air: it was only October, but the first chill of winter had begun to settle on Vermont, and the foliage had entered into its final flame of color before the barrenness of deep cold. I was always struck by the strange irony of autumn—for only in their penultimate descent to death do the leaves reveal their most sublime texture. It is as though the saturated cherry-red and the tangerine fire each were held deep within—concealed in the soul of the leaf. And as the leaf prepares to die, to yield to the relentless winds of approaching frost, it starts to show its true face, the essence of its beauty. Is our deepest self opened up as we approach the end? Is there anything sublime in it for us whatsoever?

In from the wondrous chill, passing the bell tones of the porch wind chime, into the main house. I remember the intimacy and romance of hushed voices, the white linen tablecloths, the gleam of lamps against window glass in the dining room. There was a pumpkin brie bisque, elegant lettuce greens, sweet onions, tomatoes ripe with flavor, rich balsamic vinaigrette. In the afternoons, hot apple cider and cinnamon cookies in the sun-washed parlor. There were walks along the property—mornings after a late breakfast—first the gravel road, then the grass hills that descended into wooded paths. There were morning drives into the neighboring towns, a day trip to Brattleboro, where we wandered around musty antique shops and down sidewalks in the breeze with palms pressed together. Arriving and departing, there were the hills of shifting color and streams of roving light.

17

Endings

Wednesday evening: 6:30 p.m.

Rabbi Hammerman enters Leah's room with us; we have asked him to guide us through the *vidui* ritual—the final confession to God before death, the prayer for forgiveness of a person's lifetime of sins. Rabbi Hammerman is a close family friend—he conducted Leah's bat mitzvah some twenty years ago, and he was one of the rabbis who officiated at our wedding.

He speaks to her—a small black prayer book in his hand.

Can she hear him? Can she hear us?

I lead the last part of the ritual—the final recitation of the *Shema*, the biblical words that the ancient Rabbi Akiva famously uttered with his last breath: *Hear, O Israel, the Lord our God, the Lord is One....* My voice is trembling and breaking; my eyes cannot contain the free-flowing grief.

It is then that I remove the wedding ring from Leah's finger (*Do you remember, love? There, under a canopy of promises . . .*)—physical symbol of our approaching separation, of the abyss that has already begun to divide us. Upon returning home, I put her ring on a holder we received as an engagement gift and place it on the mantle. I can't help wondering: How long will I continue to wear my own wedding ring when hers has been removed? Is it loyalty?

Mist at Morro Bay

Memory? Is it my desire to still be enveloped in the traces of her touch?

The *Shema* before death: eyes closed like the *Shema* we recited in bed each night with Aderet. These are the last words on our lips before the unconsciousness of sleep descends; and they are the last words on our lips before consciousness disappears forever, before the last inhalation and exhalation of breath.

> *Fishbane family, good night.*
> *Imma, good night.*

The dying person emulates the ancient sage, the ancient martyr: the words mark a final devotion to God—a love that is not even diminished in the face of deep suffering.

But like so many others, Leah cannot speak in her last moments; and so I become the mouthpiece of her final confession, the conduit for her last words. I proclaim God's unity for her: the inseparability of her presence and her absence courses through me like a fierce stream. She is here in the words that I speak, and yet I know that she is already gone.

∽

I return to the hospital well before dawn on Thursday.

After a few hours of rest at home, I am on my way back—through the empty silence of blackened streets. A quiet wrapped in the midnight cold—ice-covered pathways, and roads dark with a barrenness unseen in the day. As I walk from the car to the hospital doors, I can feel the thin freeze of the air washing through my throat and lungs. The solitude of this hour of night feels both ominous and otherworldly; I can almost see myself moving about as a lost figure of shadows, the thick warmth of my breath hanging in the air like the remnants of a dream. The chill passes through me, and I remember.

Back in the ICU, I find Barbara and Jack still there— exhausted from having stayed by Leah's side through the night. I ask them if they managed any sleep. They didn't go home at all to rest?

We'll take what we can get, Jack says in a voice that reveals a parent's broken heart.

Later they would tell me: *We did not want her to be alone; we couldn't bear to leave her there alone . . .*

In the excruciating torment of a mother and father's collapsing world, they cry out to their child:

We're not ready for you to die . . .
Our baby . . . our little baby . . .

Leah's brother, Mitchell, and Grandma Lee take long private moments with her—in the quiet of the room they too say their final good-byes. Jack tells me that he hasn't seen his son cry like that in many years. It was always Leah who could get through to him; only she could calm him in the hours of his childhood night terrors.

I think of Leah's sister, Stephanie: she would be arriving with her husband and three kids on a flight from Florida the next afternoon. The two sisters were so close, talking on the phone two, sometimes three times a day.

And there were my parents: grieving for a woman who had also become their daughter—with a tenderness and love so unusual in an in-law relationship. And they were grieving the brokenness of their son's life, the pain that their grand-daughter was now destined to endure. Leah and my mother had developed such a close relationship; she too felt the crush of emptiness. This was one of the few times in my life that I have witnessed my father cry from deep within his heart.

The previous night I had come home to prepare Aderet for what was now understood. She deserved that much. We sit together, and I try to find the words to tell a little girl that she will never again see her mother, never again be able to feel her warm touch, to hear her voice. Once more I am searching for words in the place of no words.

Sweetheart, you know how sometimes people can get so sick that even the doctors can't make them better anymore?

Like Nana and Bapa—and they died.

Yes, love. Usually people are very old when they get that sick. But sometimes, and it doesn't happen a lot, people who are young like Imma can get so, so sick that they just can't get better anymore.

And then they die? But what kind of sick is Imma?

Imma has a special kind of sickness, sweetheart.

Much later, I overhear another child innocently ask Aderet where her mommy is now. And without hesitation, she responds: "In heaven. My Imma had a special kind of sick." I am amazed at how these words leave their mark on the mind and imagination of a little child. It wasn't until many months after this that I told Aderet what had actually caused Leah's death, on the advice of her therapist. It is important for little children to be able to name the illness, she tells me. They need to know that it's different from having a fever, from catching a cold; the people they love won't die just because they get sick.

I tell Aderet that the doctors think Imma will not get better from her sickness; they think she is going to die.

"She's going to die?" she repeats—"Oh, Imma . . . Imma!"

We hold each other. *My baby* . . .

"Abba, does that mean that Imma will have a new bed in heaven? Will Nana and Bapa be her mommy

and daddy in heaven? I think God will be her
blankie in heaven!"

And within a few moments she begins to compose drawings—notes for me to deliver to Imma on her deathbed:
one the image of her traced hand, to be placed as soothing comfort on Imma's heart. The other picture contains a
long winding line, drawn with a purple marker. When I ask
her to tell me what she has made, she says:

> *This is Imma's bed in the hospital,*
> *and this is her path to heaven.*
> *This is her bed in heaven.*

Her drawing and her narration reflect something more
profound than I could ever find the strength to say. Imma
endures beyond this bodily life; she undertakes the journey
across the threshold of time and space, from the world of
the living to the world of the dead. And even if this struc-
ture did not exist, it is willed into being by the power of a
child's imagination—it is created through the pure strength
of a daughter's love.

That's beautiful, I tell her. Imma will love it.

And with new tears beginning their descent, I hug her
tightly—I stroke her back and hair with the palm of my
hand.

Months later, looking out the car window at the bright-
blue presence above her, she says:

Abba, I think that white in the sky is God's face.
No, actually, I think it's Imma's bed up there. It's
Imma's bed in heaven. I'm sad and I love her. Abba,

I wish Imma was still in the hospital so she could come home.

~

Aderet was at home with one of my parents, or maybe she was still at school then. We were in the small room outside the ICU, the heaviness of death lingering in the air and in my deflated posture. I think this must be the room for devastated families. This is where they bring the people who need to be sheltered from the glare of the Unit, from the gaze of sympathy that follows their steps to the patient's room. This is the space where the final news of heartbreak is delivered again and again, the daily encounter with death and dying that is the work of Intensive Care.

As I step outside of myself for a fleeting moment, I wonder about the doctors and the nurses who work here—those individuals who make this ongoing journey into the burning land of suffering, trying with immense will to conquer the warrior angels of death that camp out in their hallways. Each day brings with it new battles to wage against the unyielding forces of illness and trauma, and these so often devolve into the dark lanes of mortality. I wonder what effect this daily living with death has on the men and women of the ICU—how long will they be able to bear the weight of it all? When will they want to run from the shadows of that place, to some more hopeful corner of the hospital?

I think of the little room in which we wait—how many others have sat in this antechamber of lost hope? How many other stories have unfolded and ended within these walls, and who were the people who inhabited them? Like me they have names and histories; like me they have sought to find their way out of a seemingly impenetrable blackness. They too had other friends and family to call; perhaps they also noticed the small window of this room and its gentle stream of sunlight. In this hour our tears have been emptied out; the well will soon be refilled, and we wait in the weakness of the in-between—like the slow breathing that stands on the threshold between two storm waves, like the lull in thunderclap and the drumbeat of rain in midsummer.

18

God Who Revives the Dead

Where does it end? Was I still holding on to some vague belief in bodily resurrection, some connection to the lines of Jewish liturgy repeated three times daily by traditional Jews in prayer?

> *The Faithful One who will revive the dead.*
> *Blessed are you, God, who revives the dead.*

I think of the kaddish prayer that is said only at the moment of burial:

> *May God's great name be sanctified in the world where He*
> *will one day revive the dead . . .*

If the normal mourner's kaddish includes no mention of death and dying (it is only the praising of God's name), the kaddish recited at the burial cannot escape the bluntness of that reality. This death is only for a time, the tradition tries to soothe us. It won't be long before all this pain is reversed; the One we praise daily will restore all this death back to life.

The kaddish of the burial—the prayer of one time and one place—that feels so much more true than the ordinary mourner's kaddish, the prayer that becomes the daily mantra for the bereaved. The mourner's kaddish has no room for what the griever is really feeling in those moments; it forces the mourner to proclaim God's greatness at the time when they feel it least. And that's clearly the point of the tradition: to assert a belief in the unequivocal justice of God at a moment when we cry out against the *injustice* of our pain.

I suppose many people don't really understand what they're saying anyway, or maybe the rhythms of that traditional language give comfort as a link to what our ancestors have said in response to death. The words of our fathers and mothers. But for me, the evanescent words of the burial kaddish are a little closer to the truth of feeling. To the stark reality of death and loss.

Meḥayei ha meitim—God who revives, who will revive, the dead. The language of prayer drives home the centrality of that Jewish belief. We say it over and over again in our daily prayers. Like so many others, I never believed that in its literal sense. So what does it mean? When we are so close to death, when we feel the cutting pain of loss, that hope—however irrational it may seem to us intellectually—becomes as real as anything, as powerful as our deepest prayer. And then I think: maybe it's really the mourners who need reviving; when we have descended so deeply into sorrow, the way back feels impossible—to steep, too far. Nothing short of a miracle will bring us back to life. Still, the pain that overtakes the body is as real as it gets in the journey of living—it's the ultimate sign that we ourselves aren't dead, that we have felt the immensity of love.

ᏚᎾ

I know these are the final hours. It will happen today.

Dr. H. enters the room; she tells us that she will now perform the apnea test—the final decisive indicator of brain death. First she repeats the neurological exam that I have witnessed several times: testing the pupils, water injected into the ears, reflexes, response to vigorous stimulation of the hands and feet. But nothing. No reaction, no response. They remove the automated ventilator, and squeeze air into Leah at set intervals. They are watching to see if her brain still has the ability to command breathing, to see if the brain stem has been utterly destroyed. They draw blood as they do this; they check for oxygen levels in the blood to see if there is any automatic attempt to breathe. And when the results come back, it is as we expected: no ability to breathe, no brain activity.

Empty. Empty. A bottomless hole inside of me.

As the doctor conducts the apnea test, I am holding Leah's hand in mine—I am envisioning an array of scenes from our life together; imagining that this here is our last walk together, our last journey of holding hands. I am weeping from a place so deep in my abdomen that my whole body is overtaken. It is as though a core section of my own soul is being pulled out of me, my own *neshamah*, my own spirit-breath.

And then, as the respirator is disconnected, I place my head on her chest and listen to her heartbeat until I can't hear it anymore. Is that the last pulse of life? Is it in her brain or in her heart? If this feeling in my chest is any indication, it is surely something of both. The brain may give consciousness and control of the body's function, but the heart feels like it lives on its own, the throbbing energy of life and the yearning for its return.

Her body grows cold—her lips become white, then darkened with the color of death. In accord with an ancient Jewish custom, we lift her onto blankets set out on the floor. We bend down one at a time, giving her one final kiss good-bye. We cover her with the white sheet, and I can see the pointedness of her feet on the other end. Like the gymnast she was as a child. Leah's feet.

My father and I wait in the sacred silence of that hospital room—fulfilling the religious obligation not to leave the dead unattended. Such a powerfully strange feeling to sit there with her: with her body as presence and her spirit as absence, the fragments of her departed soul strewn in the air. Am I here with her, or is she already gone? And if she is *gone*, to where does that departure lead? To the heaven of traditional belief, watching over her loves through the stars and their otherworldly lenses? To the womb of the great All of existence once again? Or is it to the empty chasm of nothingness that always seems to lie on the other side of Being and living?

We wait: waiting in the company of that which so recently held my living thinking feeling Leah. I sit there mostly unable to speak—not just because I have entered into the clouds of trauma and shock, but also out of some instinctual awareness that this is the space of ultimate silence, a domain of living that brings us to sharp encounter with the limits and edges of what it is to live. Our ability to speak, to make sense of the world, is pulled away with the speed of a magician's cloth, and all we are left with is the sensation that life's mystery exists beyond words.

If I can believe that something called *Leah* survives this (if I can believe that for even the most infinitesimal of moments), then I wonder if she has gone to a realm without words, a place without speech. Or has she perhaps not really departed at all? Does her spirit remain in our company, in the heart of her daughter, in the endurance of memories? Does she remain in me, whispering in words without sound, telling me what I must do in my moments of greatest helplessness?

Perhaps that is the most powerful gift of community and friends as we try to find our way through the unknowing ineffability of grief: in their standing before us, in their eliciting of our stories, they teach us to speak again—to rediscover the need for words as we emerge from the place of no words. From the silence of death's presence—the absence that is the most complete presence I have ever known—I pass into the muteness of life's unmaking; I travel through the mindscapes of articulation's withdrawal, through the disappearance of understanding and rational thought. I need to relearn my ability to speak as much as I must learn the ways of a single parent.

We wait there, in the stillness of the room. We wait in the liminal space of the speechless. We wait until the gruff men from the funeral home arrive with the gurney and the body bag. A crimson cloth bag with a long zipper, harnessed onto the rolling gurney. My father tells me that he will accompany Leah in the hearse; he will make sure for me that she is treated gently and with great respect. I watch, stunned, as they take her away to the waiting car—I hold my coat and hat in my shaking hands.

From that moment on, and perhaps from well before, I experience my surroundings as through a dense cloud.

Things appear to be happening around me, but I don't really see them and I don't really care. I sit and walk with an immense weakness, as though all the energy and vitality have been drained out of me. I cannot lift my eyes to meet the person who seeks to greet and console me. I move about with eyes cast to the ground; I can barely acknowledge the presence of others beside me. All, that is, except for Aderet. As soon as I hear her voice, it pierces the fog that envelops me—I am awakened and immediately aware of her.

We sit in a large room prior to the service, and scores of people come up to us, one by one, each offering a small measure of consolation—words of love, an embrace around the neck. My eyes are glazed over with tears, and I hold Aderet close to me. To sit there alone would be unbearable.

Face after face; many from our current community, some from long ago. But it is when Robin, Aderet's pre-school teacher, reaches us that my weeping opens up again from its deep place. Something in her tenderness toward Aderet rips open my heart—the knowledge that she would be a daily witness to my daughter's grieving, a physical reminder of the world-shattering unfairness of our new life.

And there she lies: concealed now in the wood that will hold her within the soil, still draped in the dark velvet cloth, marked with the Jewish Star of David. Aderet and I give Leah one last kiss through that garment:

That's Imma's bed, she says.
I love you, Imma. Good-bye, Imma.

19

Shivah

During shivah I experience my whole self as dazed and slow:
it is as though a fog of unknowing has descended onto my
consciousness of the world around. I tell the story of Leah's
death over and over again, to almost every cluster of people
that walk in the door, that sit in my living room—early in
the morning after removing the tefillin from my head and
arm, in the late morning as I drink yet another cup of coffee,
in the afternoon and early evening as crowds of people enter
my home to be with me for the *minḥah* and *ma'ariv* prayer
services, for my recitation of the kaddish along with other
members of the family.

And the telling itself becomes a kind of mantra in my
wilderness: it brings me back from the anchorless drift of a
grieving stupor, connects me to Leah and our shared story
again and again. With each telling I hear myself begin to
formulate a narrative that repeats: words, phrases, stages of
narration. That was the start of my storytelling: the same
impulse that would drive me toward the desire to write
about it so soon after. I feel myself wrapped in the act of
storytelling—the narration becomes like a warm blanket
in this bone-chilling cold. And as I tell the tale again and
again, my eyes are fixed away from the listeners—fixed
in a daze on the hardwood planks of the floor. As each
person comes to greet me, I speak to them with eyes cast

away—I cannot bring myself to receive the direct light of another person's face.

I sit in the living room of our house—the house that we bought and moved into only nine months before—and I am surrounded by the comfort of so many well-wishers, some who have traveled from across the country, my aunt from Israel, and of course the streams of kind faces from our new community in New Jersey. The immensity of their hearts still moves me. Each day there are new platters of food being delivered, new acts and offers of kindness—the wonder and strength of community to step in when we are most helpless, when we are the most fragile.

It was in that space of fragility and weakness that several moms in the neighborhood organized Aderet's princess birthday party—re-placed from our house and the space of mourning to our next-door neighbor's home. Even now, especially now, Aderet should have the joy of being a birthday princess, and in much the same way that Leah had planned it. Leah died on a Thursday, and Aderet's fourth birthday party had been scheduled for the upcoming Sunday. Leah had planned it down to the last detail: the princess theme, the arts-and-crafts supplies that she had ordered, the balloons and the cake. And in the end I couldn't bear to take that joy away from my little girl: her corner of happiness in the middle of so much sadness and so much heartache.

It is the first in a long stream of moments in which Leah will be absent. The ordinary treasures of life's passing reel. I think of the way Aderet will always feel this absence—at every transition in her childhood and adulthood: graduations, a bat mitzvah, a wedding . . . And in this moment I recognize a feeling that will be with us from here on out: happiness inseparable from pain, the bitter and the sweet becoming one. I smile when the women tell me of their plans; they will videotape the party for me to watch when I am ready. Just as the funeral was videotaped for Aderet to watch when she is older.

In the house of shivah there is still the sound of children playing, and I am grateful for that: Aderet's cousins who have come in from Florida run about with a sweet purity. They create their own space of imaginative games together—their own little circle of love and comfort within a sea of pain and weeping adults. And the bighearted character of this community is my redemption in miniature—I know now that without all these hands to hold me up—to hold *us* up—I would have fallen further into the abyss of darkness that was constantly pulling at me from below.

20

Kaddish

And again—kaddish.

According to traditional Jewish law, a spouse says kaddish only for the first thirty days following the burial (the *shloshim*), whereas a child says the kaddish for almost an entire year upon the death of her parent. This distinction hadn't even occurred to me before I lost Leah, and as I began the process of mourning I assumed that I too would be saying the kaddish for a full year. How could I have imagined anything different? Hadn't we too become as one blood and one flesh? For if the kaddish is the external marker of my Jewish mourning, then would its cessation be some kind of formal relinquishing of my state of feeling, some outer threshold in my grief?

Someone recently told me of a well-known and much-revered Orthodox rabbi who said kaddish for his wife for three and a half years—as if in overt testimony to the artificiality of setting time limits on the external road of mourning. If I acquiesce to the brevity of the thirty days, does that somehow proclaim that I am no longer a mourner? I almost see this in the way people perceive me now.

"You are looking so much better," one friend says to me—comparing my demeanor now to the way I was in the first days and weeks. And I suppose I am doing better. Better than I was. I am able to laugh now; I can function with greater ease in social situations. But what does this signify to the others that I meet? Should I still be unable to laugh? Should my voice still tremble when I speak? Should I cast my eyes away?

Rising to say the kaddish each day of the first month, joining the company of other mourners who stand as part of the communal choreography of grief and remembrance, I first hold the prayer book and gaze at the shape of the words on the page. In those first weeks my mind is still shrouded in the deep fog of the unsteady hours. And soon I feel the need to close my eyes as I say it, to put my prayer book down on the seat, to remove myself from the visual space in which I stand. Then there is only the rhythm of the word-sounds, the Aramaic hymn to God's majesty and exaltation (is that what I feel?), the tones and chorus of other mourners—the faces of others erased for the brief moment of complete inwardness. When she wants to be there, Aderet is in my arms, her head on my shoulder. But most of the time she is a bouncy, sparkling four-year-old, running about the shul with her friends while I enter into the cadence of my returning liturgy:

> *Yitgadal ve-yitkadash she-mei rabbah . . .*
> *May God's great name be exalted and sanctified . . .*
>
> *Be-alma divra khirutei ve-yamlikh malkhutei . . .*
> *In the world that He created according to His will and in*
>   *which His kingship will reign . . .*

Eyes closed again, hand on the chair to keep me steady—words in darkness, sounds surrounding the memories of Leah conjured in the lens of my mind. And now, even though I no longer go to shul daily to utter the kaddish, I still cannot bring myself to stop completely. When I come on Shabbat, and it is time for the mourners to rise and say their kaddish, I too rise in the communal theatrics of grief, and I too say the words again. I am still a mourner, I tell myself. I have not yet reached the end of my grieving—not even that part which is exposed in the public space of community.

"Abba," she says, "when I'm older will you teach me how to say the kaddish? Because I want to say my kaddish for Imma."

Again I remember saying the burial kaddish at Leah's grave on the day of the funeral. I still have the white note card with the text printed on it in stark black lettering. It bears a smudge, an earth stain from my fingertips when they still carried traces of her grave soil. Crouching by the filled-in grave on that day, I had picked up a bit of the dirt that now completes her space; I rolled it between my fingertips. I remember feeling that this was my last touch of her presence in the hour of her leaving—it was the fullness of earth-memory: the return dust of before and after. At shul, a friend tells me that as Leah's grave was filled in, I appeared to stand there as the human marker of her place in the ground, emerging from the soil as the living stone of Leah's memory, hand held tightly to my eyes and forehead. I can see, and I can hear: the sound of the shovelfuls of soil beating the wood of the pine coffin like the thunderous second hand of time's universal clock. I know this will be: transmitting to Aderet the presence of her mother, telling and retelling the story of Leah, carrying her inside through all the hours that are still to come.

21

A Visit to the Doctor

I go to my internist—the congestion in my chest has persisted for more than two weeks now, and I am finally motivated to do something about it. But when he enters the examination room and sits down, I realize that he does not know about Leah; he does not know what has really been going on with me these last months. When he asks how I am doing and I tell him (I mean *really tell him*), I can see the usual brevity of examination and diagnosis slip away—almost as though he realizes that the healing I have come for is far more than antibiotics for the chest.

He is deeply compassionate, and then reveals to me that he too went through an almost identical ordeal some five years ago. His wife also died suddenly, leaving him with his bottomless grief and a young daughter to care for on his own. He sits with me for several long minutes, listening to my story, and then telling me his own. With a gentle voice, he shares with me his path from total despair to some measure of redemption. He asks if he can give me a hug. I realize as I leave the office, a prescription for Azithromycin in my hands, that this time I received much more than I came in for—more than I was expecting.

22

Into Spring

May has arrived with all its promise and verdant unfolding. The dark-red buds in the front yard have begun to emerge: they drink in spring's magical alternation between rain-wash and sun-stream. The days are still comfortable—cool in the morning, not yet the oppressive heat of the summer months. Still on leave from work, I try to get out of the house at least once each day—sometime during the hours before I will need to pick Aderet up from her preschool. And though I feel I have begun to adjust to my newfound responsibilities as a single father, I quickly become exhausted from the weight of it all. It's not just the draining nature of having to do the work of two parents—it's the inexplicable heaviness that I still carry. The feeling that Aderet's entire fate, her whole well-being, rests on me: at the end of the day there is no one else. Not grandparents, not friends—though everyone tries so hard to help us—it is just us two now, father and daughter.

Aderet's teacher gently reminds me that Mother's Day is coming soon: they will be doing projects in class; they will be talking about the love of children for their mothers. *What should they do?* she asks me. *We can avoid it altogether with the kids—just say the word.* I say that Aderet will want to make pictures for her Imma; she will want to talk about it, to say out loud how much she still loves her. And as it approaches, she scribbles little notes to Leah on heart-shaped pieces of paper, placing them carefully and systematically in a series of pouches set out in the living room. When she dictates one to me, I transcribe it—fixing it on the fridge with a magnet:

> *I love you, Imma,*
> *I can't wait for Mother's Day.*
> *I got bears for you at the toy store—*
> *A yellow one and a pink one:*
> *They say "I love you, Mom."*

The manifestations of her grief continue to surprise me: the ways she seeks to express herself reveal thoughts that simmer beneath the surface. At the Shabbat table this week Aderet pours water into a bowl, mixing it with salt—she is absorbed in a world of imaginative creation, the reinvention of rituals.

> *These are the salty tears,* she says.
> *Salty tears for Imma. 'Cause we're so sad about Imma.*

As I tuck her in for the night, my child asks me for another story. And she tells me what she wants: in this one Imma will be alive; we will all be together again—Imma, Abba, and Aderet. She turns to me (perhaps she senses my pause), and she says:

> *It's okay to pretend that your Imma is alive, even when she*
> *is really dead.*
> *Yes, sweetheart. Of course.*

I think again of the flowers she wants to put on "Imma's bed" at the cemetery. And I wonder when we will have the strength to do that, when I will even have the strength to go: flowers for Imma, Aderet's small hand in my own—her orphaned pain locked in my heart.

I didn't expect Mother's Day to be particularly hard— as a part of the calendar it always seemed perfectly random to me, invented by the greeting-card industry. But now the day is coming to a slow close, and I identify the pangs of grief swelling my insides. I linger over a framed eight-by-ten-inch photo that stands in my bedroom—a picture of Leah and Aderet in our backyard in Los Angeles, sunshine and cool shadow enveloping their faces in the luminous Southern California morning. What I love about this picture is how wondrously real Leah looks in it: in her body's gesture, in the openness of her face—she is just so much *herself*, so much as I remember her in her time of vibrance, in her time of life. Holding the frame close as I lie in bed, I can almost feel her presence again, I can almost hear her voice—just as it was, *just as it was.*

23

The Path We Travel

The way forward: what does it hold for us?
Is there any redemption, or are we now the ones exiled
    from love?

Lost together in the dark plains of terrifying expanse,
wandering together in the shallow waters of unsurpassable
horizons, in the caves of endlessly echoing sound.
    All at once I understand the words of the psalmist:

> *I lift up my eyes to the mountains—*
> *From where will my help come?*

But unlike the psalmist I see no answer to the question, no
divine resolution in the desperation of quiet loneliness.
    In this valley of winding paths, we still search for a trail
out of the darkness.

Aderet and I are sitting at the kitchen table; she has just
returned from spending two days with Grandma and
Grandpa. "Abba," she says, "my heart's broken when I miss
you. And you know also why my heart is broken? Because
Imma died, and I miss her. She was alive for a very long
time, it seems! But I miss her, and I feel in my heart that I
love her." She begins to sing . . . "And good night, Imma, I
really miss you . . . And I want you to wake up again for a
minute, and even for more than a minute. And I would like

you to stay up and talk to me . . . We will have so much fun, and we will talk and talk the whole entire night, and we will talk and play and camp out in the darkness . . ."

In time—*in time,* they say.

But it is time itself that is flipped on its head in these rooms that grief has made. For all my attempts to recover the sequence of events that has led us to this moment, to chronicle the road in and out of sorrow, I have come to know time in a way that seems to resist the usual, linear progression of hours and days. For I find that grief is not always linear: memory returns with its unpredictable cycles; the events and thoughts that will trigger the heartache once again—they cannot be anticipated, they cannot be planned for.

I discover that my mind has been set adrift from what we ordinarily expect from time and progress. The straight lines and forward motion of experience are replaced with a most strange sense of disorder, the weave of consciousness overtaken by circles of intersecting memory, longing, and the slow first steps of hope.

Father and daughter, into journeys unknown:
Somehow, from out of this unending night, we will find
    our way.

24

Letters in the Dark

It's been more than two months now, and I've been watching the seasons: winter-spring, now signs of summer. There will be the recession of May, the thick heat of July reawakened.

And all around me are the flames of spring in the month of emerging buds: nature's rapid rebirth.

This regeneration of life, this reincarnation out of winter's cold death: it is the other to our human fate, not to rise again or to be reborn from the unstoppable stillness.

So I observe the full force of this season's unveiling: white and pink bleeding hearts on our front lawn, the flower whose texture speaks nature's language of memory and forgetting, whose form captures the ebb of our forsaken hope even as it promises restoration.

The shape of its growth, the vivid flow of its color, a revelation of the deep patterns of love and the broken heart, emblems engraved into the table of being, reflections of our fragile humanness—this bleeding sadness of ours.

And there are the azaleas in their wild magenta passion, coming up out of the stark barrenness into the lush eros of summer's edge: so many buds, so much rebirth.

∽

I realize the extent to which your expressions and mannerisms have entered into me, have become my own. Now as natural to me as my own instincts, I discover the traces of your living presence surfacing in those unexpected moments.

And I think of how with the passage of time we came to know each other's thoughts and reservations—sentences finished and reactions synchronized—the sharing of a mind and a heart.

These days Aderet asks me "to make the faces Imma used to make"—and I think this is her own fear of forgetting, of wanting to stave off the inevitable fading of your presence. Of course, it's so clear how deeply you are woven into her, but it is the familiarity of your gestures that she is desperate not to lose.

And I am desperate too. I make the faces and I call up the memories that come with them. The playful ones and the sad ones—those that others knew, and those that were our secret family language.

I remember how I used to wonder just how real my life was—what proof did I have that all this was not the mere dream of some divine mind, that I wasn't an unreal figment of that colossal imagination? And these days I am thinking these bizarre thoughts once again. Perhaps all this misery and all this solitude are nothing but a stream of the unconscious.

But I don't really have the luxury of these meditations for long. Aderet brings me back—the simple earthiness of her play brings me back, and my sharp ache for you brings me back to the sobriety and world-boundedness of daily life.

∽

This morning I'm missing your voice, the ordinary gestures of your presence.

And the absence that is more real than anything else—
it leaves me disoriented and afraid: lost.

How does the shape of a whole life disappear in an
instant? How do we wake together one morning only to
watch you slip away the next?

Walking in the supermarket the other afternoon,
I almost thought I saw you in the next aisle—you were
pushing Aderet in the shopping cart the way you always
did, your hair and your neck were just as I knew them, just
as I remember them.

Did I really expect to see you there? I wonder if my
imagination and my dreams can will you back to life, can
call you back to the way you were then.

∽

I finally found you there, your corner of space in that
crowded terrain of death.

This way, 'migo, the cemetery gardener says to me. *Over
there.*

It's warm today, and the sun is bright.

Three and a half months it took me, but today when I
woke I knew all of a sudden; all at once I was filled with the
desire, with the need, to visit your grave.

It is a vast, empty space; the markers of other memories all around, names of other lives and the small stones
placed there by the survivors, by the ones whose fate it is
to remember.

Your space there is so much smaller than I remember—
on that day, with so many other people standing beside
me, with the space expanded by the tent overhead. Now I

kneel beside you, and the earth still looks so fresh: a mixture of soil and gravel-rock; the tiny patches of grass struggling to form themselves over the rupture in the expanse of meadow. And all that stands to distinguish your place amid this massive city of the dead is a low marker, placed there on the day we buried you, after the grave was filled in:

Leah Levitz Fishbane
September 7, 1974–March 1, 2007

Your dad told me that he would like to put up a headstone as soon as possible, and I understand now what he meant: it's just so fragile there, and so fresh. You've been left there untouched since our parting—not even the top layer of your earth-blankets has been moved. And I think of all the weather that has passed since that day—snow and rain and stifling heat.

I have brought letters to read to you, to your presence that hears and does not hear. As on the day of your burial, I hold a pinch of your grave-soil between my thumb and forefinger; I hold a tiny piece of rock and then I return it to its place. There is no one else here on this hot Friday afternoon, and I lie down beside you on the grass, imagining that we are once again lying next to each other in our bedroom, or in the sun of an outdoor picnic. In this place I listen to the quiet of speechless lands—all these markers of remembered love, all these routes of return into the regions of living memory.

Lying next to Aderet at bedtime, I read her the story of the acorn and its long journey to become an oak. From seed to sapling to grown tree, and finally the ineluctable death of that living form: the return of what was vibrant to the ground of the earth, the energy of the once living tree now serving as the source from which new things may grow, from which new trees may be planted.

Oh, love. Your presence is here—I can feel it, and your voice resounds in my head. The turns of your face rise from my own facial memory, from my own skin. You are there, inside of me, the texture of my body's wordless past.

Again I say the kaddish, my words now audible only to this quorum of graves—spoken only to you as my substitute for speech, as the slow hew of form in the limitless quarry of silence.

I will be back. I blow a kiss and I take in one last look. I will come back to you here, my love.

∽

Passage between states of relation: single, married, and back again. From two separate people, destinies unbound, to become that merged identity of family—the new life we created from our own flesh: anticipation, memory, hope.

Love: I am thinking about us now, the *us* that I still cannot help saying—our house, our friends, our daughter. Our bed.

Not long after you died, and I referred to it as *Imma and Abba's*, Aderet corrected me in a way that only she could: "It's not Imma's bed anymore, Abba. It's only your bed now."

I don't remember if she said it then, but I know she thinks it now: your bed is in heaven—concealed in the cloud-house of visible days. Swinging in the backyard, her head turned up, she says, "Abba, are you looking at Imma too? Are you looking at her house in the sky? The cloud is her house in heaven, and her bed is inside."

Your repose in the hospital flew skyward when you died, like the magical beds that flew in the created world of Márquez, alive during the summer we traveled through France together, each reading a copy of *One Hundred Years of Solitude*. I still recall the otherworldly texture of that book, its ascent beyond the ridges of time, the feeling of lying next to you in that Avignon hotel, both of us absorbed in the joined world of solitude's senses, and yet both calm in the presence of shared space and unuttered words.

So have I now crossed back over the threshold of my individuality, from *Eitan and Leah* to *Eitan alone*? Surely it is not now as it once was—how could it be? I can't recover the first innocence that I long for, remote in some inaccessible region of my past, in some withdrawn space of my inwardness. What becomes of my individuality now? What is the shape of me in this terrain of undefined futures?

Already I imagine the interior of your memory, kept like sacred shards in the box of my returning gaze.

I don't think we can ever really get it back, that stillness before life's undoing, that space when everything was laid out before us like a map of untraveled wonders. But here, in the darkness, I will carry you in the vault of weightlessness into new lands unsettled in my mind—for the blessing of memory and the memory of blessing.

25

The Shape of Survival

It's hard to believe that more than six months have passed. Some days the whole thing still feels unreal; other times the steady weight of awareness settles in, and it occurs to me that this is what life has dealt me. This is the inescapable reality of our days.

On Rosh ha-Shanah I stand and chant the liturgy that speaks so bluntly about mortality—of our living and our dying. Who will live and who will die this year?

Who will be inscribed in the Book of Life?
The human being is dust, and it is to dust that she will
    return.

As I recite these words my inner eye flashes to the visage of Leah's grave, of me seated on the grass beside that place on the afternoon before *Rosh ha-Shanah*.

Dust to dust.

I try to speak to her in this space, but I can feel her returning to the earth.

Six months.

All at once I am aware that this time has proven to be a process of evolution for me, the slow rebirth of my self from the embers of a violent fire. At this moment I am aware of my first steps along a path of a new kind of walking. I think of those magical days when Aderet was taking her first steps in our California living room—toddling a few paces and then falling down again. That's me.

I hear my therapist's voice. *You're doing okay, Eitan.* Think of how proud of you Leah would be—if she could see you functioning as a single parent without completely losing your cool, mastering the art of packing lunches for school and getting the little princess out the door in the morning. Think of her voice and her expression if she could see you cooking Shabbat dinner for the first time in, well, a long time. *Sweetie, look at you!* she would say. And then I can hear her become playful again: *So how come you couldn't do this when I was around?*

I return in my mind to that Shabbat lunch three weeks after Leah's death, my parents ready to leave the next day for Chicago. They had to go back to their lives and work, and I had to prepare myself for this new aloneness, now even more complete. All at once it hit me that my new life as a single father was about to begin in earnest. Everything that needed doing would now be my responsibility. Mine alone.

And for a long while it was just the comfort of simple routines. I would take Aderet to her preschool only six blocks from home (this after the early-morning rush of fixing breakfast, making and packing her lunch, moving through the rhythms of tooth brushing and getting dressed), then eventually heading back out for my one out-of-the-house activity for the day. Usually it was my drive over to the bookstore-café—a place where I could feel the comfort of other people all around me, and yet still be secluded in the solitude of my writing notebook and my cup of cinnamon tea.

Early on it was the writing in that pocket notebook that gave me a stable anchor of return—its cover textured with an imitation-leather design of gold and red, the perfect feel of my favorite pen between my fingers and on the paper. Even then I could feel the power of that writing to keep me afloat, to channel the depths into graspable words, to release the fierce energy of pain in confession and poetry—even if it flowed out only to come back again with seemingly renewed force. But I now think that it ebbed more and more slowly until I had to stop, until my heart needed to rest.

But even more it was the openhearted love of my community here, and especially the handful of families who took us in, week in and week out. Several nights a week Aderet and I were invited over to nearby friends—and as much as it was the gift of food, it was the gift of companionship that held the most power in surviving those dark times. A friend here affirmed my need to write about the pain, as well as my desire to share it with others. For the one who suffers does not seek a quick fix for the torment. Instead, the griever needs someone to *hold* his pain: to take in some measure of it, to listen, to embrace.

If I can identify one thing that has helped me survive these last months, it is that: in carrying us when we are at our weakest, true friendship and community step into the breach to hold our pain. It is a holding that is not a transfer of suffering, but a *being present* that is embodied in the one who comes to hold the mourner's hand in silence.

Sometimes there are no words worthy of being said—then it is just the company of another person, there to hold us in our darkest place, to keep our heads above water until we are strong enough to do it ourselves.

And as I remember my passage through the Jewish rituals of mourning, surrounded as I was by the warmth and love of a caring community, I realize that these structures of time come to us from the tradition as a buffer against the tidal waves of crushing solitude. From within those walls of grief's terrain, I hear the ancient words recited to me again and again:

> *Ha-Makom Yenaḥeim etkhem be-tokh she'ar aveilei tzion*
> *vi-yerushalayim—*
> May God comfort you among all the other
>   mourners of Zion and Jerusalem.

Comfort within the fellowship of those who have experienced this pain themselves. For who else could really understand us? Who could fathom our pain and our despair?

The name used for God in this traditional formula sets me to thinking. *Ha-Makom*—simply, "The Place"—one of those recurrent names for God used in classical rabbinic literature. God as Place. Indeed, the Place of all places—the cosmic space in which this world is inscribed and enfolded. And despite this global image, I think the real power of *Makom* is far more local. It is the *Makom* of community; the *Makom* of the shul where we meet our friends and call up the power to pray; the *Makom* of this house where Leah's traces are so present. For as I can believe that God is to be found in everyday reality—not secluded above in the transcendent heavens—I find that Presence, that divine indwelling, in the ordinary and extraordinary acts of kindness that have been given to me these last months.

A teacher of mine who visited the house during shivah said: "I would say *Ha-Makom Yenaḥeim*, but I really think *Ha-Zman Yenaḥeim*—that Time will bring comfort." He too offered that play on words as a fragment of hope.

God as Place. God as Time.

The healing power of time's passage is itself a divine manifestation—we put the pieces of a broken life back together as best we can, and each moment is layered on top of the others, each day building to the slow crossing of unforeseen thresholds. But as I think of these months gone by, and of our attempt to cut a path in the thorny brush of a dark wilderness, I am drawn again to this image of Place—to God as the energy that underlies the space of community, Divinity whose rays of light are revealed to the sufferer through the words and hands of friendship.

In the symbolic language of Jewish mysticism, the *Shekhinah* (the feminine divine presence, the tenth emanative stream within the One God that is closest to our human world) is often represented by the term *Kenesset Yisrael*, "The Assembly (or Community) of Israel." In its kabbalistic context, *Kenesset Yisrael* refers to a heavenly dimension of God, the earthly terminology but a symbolic marker for an otherworldly meaning. But today I want to read it much more literally. That dimension of God that is most associated with an Indwelling in the human world; that part of Divinity that is most revealed to human consciousness—it is manifest and present in the living breath of community. The community that takes care of its weakest in their times of need and desperation; the community that works divine miracles in bringing fragments of light to those who are submerged in the darkest of spaces.

That is creation, revelation, and redemption bound up in One—all of those divine forces show themselves in the working of community to lift up the fallen, to bring comfort to those whose spirits have been ground into the dust. That, I believe, is the true meaning of *Ha-Makom Yenaḥeim*— in and through the places where we are, where we suffer, and where we begin to rise. It is in that getting up—the elevation that can come only through the loving hands of friendship—it is there that the ultimate reconstruction of *divine* space (*Makom*) can begin. Indeed, it is the repair and the rebuilding of God's own broken self—the divine face shattered like the first vessels of creation, fragments that reflect the pain and the broken heart of this world. But the pieces are melded back together, even if they can never be the Whole that they once were. For it is also a world of love: a place where simple acts of kindness and generosity have the power to bring redemption—to redeem the person bound in the chains of despair.

∽

Today, as I drive into the city, the morning is clear and bright—the transcendent air of fall is awake and brilliant. Summer is over, and we are suspended in the eternal return of the Jewish holidays—between Rosh ha-Shanah and Yom Kippur, the smell of Sukkot and its pine-green joy palpable on the edges. As I come off the bridge and turn onto the West Side Highway, the Hudson River is revealed as an incandescent reflection; vivid and radiant on this September morning, it is a reminder to me that the sun will continue to rise, that the river will be there to receive it.

And so I take in this brief eruption of the sublime. I have returned to teaching, and it is good: back into the life I have made, the life that Leah helped me build. One step, and then another.

Inaudible, I speak a prayer: a prayer that knows this pain will become more bearable with time; that just as I have crossed this first seemingly infinite horizon, so too there will be more to come—each day a threshold, each day another healing salve for a soul on its way back to the world of the living.

Afterword

As I write these words, more than four years have passed since Leah's death. Some days it seems like ages ago; on others I am right back there, absorbed into the trauma. I realize that this is a lifelong process—a pain that never disappears completely, even if the frequency and the depth of the suffering are eased. An unanticipated trigger can bring it all tumbling back. I have heard that this can happen decades after the fact, even as life has taken on new dimensions of happiness and fulfillment.

Most of this book was written in the first six months amid a kind of creative fury—a time that seemed to open into an altered state of perception, and in which I felt possessed by the speech of grieving, by a need to get it out onto paper. I identify with the way poet and memoirist Mark Doty characterized this in the opening pages of his remarkable *Heaven's Coast*:

> Almost eighteen months after Wally died, I know a little differently. I see a little more broadly than the man who wrote these pages, adrift in the sea-swirl of shock and loss. But something's gained by allowing the voice of those hours, the long days of new mourning, to have its say. In a way I know less now, too. The Lakota Sioux say that when nature gives

one a burden, one's also given a gift. Loss brought with it a species of vision, an inwardness which was the gift of a terrible time—nearly unbearable, but bracingly real. I felt I was breathing some strange new air, the dizzy-making oxygen of an unfamiliar altitude.

I too stand in a different place than I did four years ago. I probably could not write these pages the same way now as I did then. But I think there is something powerful in that, something that is inexpressible from the place of distance. The searing heat of the first months of mourning is an experience that must be expressed—and perhaps only from within the storm. For that too is an inescapably real aspect of our humanity—one that needs to be heard and held.

It is a hand extended to those who are now wading through the long and lonely hours, and it is a kind of confession that reaches out for the gift and compassion of witnessing. I hope most of all that my words reach those of you who are carrying the heavy weight of mourning: that my own retelling may allow you to know that you are not alone in this unbearable pain; that although each of us travels a road that is unique in its suffering and memory, there is a community of friends and strangers who share an experience that cannot be known from the outside—only embraced in empathy.

Aderet will soon be starting third grade and is growing in ways I couldn't have dreamed of four years ago. She has traveled her own road of healing—a journey that will no doubt take many different forms throughout her life. Thank you, sweet girl, for giving my life purpose these last years, for blessing me with the strength of your love. I hope that these pages give you some comfort and company in the years ahead, a glimpse of your life before memory. I am grateful every day to be your father, and this book is dedicated to you with the deepest love.

Hard to imagine four years ago, I can now say that I have been blessed to find new love: I remarried last summer. I am filled with gratitude to now share my life journey with Rabbi Julia Andelman—for the patience and kindness that are so deeply found in her. It is no easy thing to marry a widower, to love a man who has been through this kind of trauma. It takes a very special person to open her heart amid such an emotional minefield, and I want to recognize the extraordinary way in which Julia has done that—opening her love to me and to Aderet, my child who has been so hungry for a mother's love. As we set out together on this path, I look forward to many years of joy and shared purpose, to the adventures waiting on the road ahead.

To my parents, Mona and Michael Fishbane: Your love and support these last years have been immeasurably meaningful to me. You have given of yourselves with extraordinary generosity, even through your own pain. I remain forever grateful for the way you have stood by us in this time of suffering, and I am honored to call myself your son.

The support we have received from family and friends, from the moment of Leah's death through the time that I am writing these words, has been staggering. I couldn't possibly succeed in thanking every person who reached out to us, so I fear I will inevitably overlook someone in this accounting.

Nevertheless, I would be more than remiss if I didn't at least try to list the many wonderful people who have given of themselves. My deep thanks to

> Barbara and Jack Levitz—we have grieved in different ways, but you have amazed me with the strength and depth of your character, and I cherish having you in our lives
>
> Lee Gibbs, Mitchell Levitz, Stephanie and David Englander, and the Englander cousins—we are blessed to have such loving and caring family
>
> Elisha and Tzippy Russ-Fishbane, and the Russ-Fishbane cousins—for the calls and the concern, even when I didn't have the strength to respond; your love and kindness mean so much to us
>
> Janet "Nanny" DeKoven—you are a treasure and a model to us all
>
> Sidra DeKoven Ezrahi—deep thanks for all of your generous efforts to help me get this book into view
>
> Amy and Chanan Vogel—for uncountable Shabbat meals and astonishing generosity; you have redefined the ideal of a caring neighbor
>
> Rachel Rittberg Abramson and Ami Abramson—for your open hearts and your boundless gifts of food and friendship
>
> Shelley Kniaz and Eliezer Diamond—for the comfort you gave us, and for our Wednesday-night dinners
>
> Rachel Lendner
>
> Risa Agin Levin and Daniel Levin

Martha and Dori Resnick

Leah and Ira Zaretsky

Debbi Bohnen and Adam Wall

Lisanne and David Cheifetz

Amy and Scott Bolton

Kenneth Berger

Leon Kass—for your great generosity in helping me first navigate the mysterious world of publishing

Jonathan Sarna

Nessa Rapoport

Hope Edelman

Dani Shapiro

Nehemia Polen

Linda Raphael

Sharon Brous

Bernie McGinn

Mychal Springer

The anonymous readers for the press

Bill Cutter

Neil Gillman

Burt Visotzky

Barry Lichtenberg—friend and fellow traveler on this road

Adam Rubin

Philip Shakhnis and Deena Weisbaum

Deborah and Chaim Singer-Frankes

Andrea Hodos and Aryeh Cohen

Bill Lebeau

Tom Fields-Meyer

The many therapists, schoolteachers, and summer-camp staff who have been so supportive and helpful in this journey.

My colleagues and the administration of the Jewish Theological Seminary, so many of whom expressed great kindness and compassion—for the patience you showed me as I gradually returned to work

Congregation Beth Sholom in Teaneck, New Jersey— you have shown me the redemptive power of community

Let me conclude with a few words of gratitude to the folks at Syracuse University Press. First and foremost, my sincere appreciation to Annelise Finegan for first welcoming and guiding this project with thoughtfulness and sensitivity. Thanks as well to Lynn Hoppel for her splendid artistic talent in designing the cover, Victoria Lane for a beautiful interior design, Mona Hamlin for her devoted work in publicity, Annette Wenda for her careful and considerate copyediting, and Mary Selden Evans, Kay Steinmetz, and the rest of the wonderful staff at the press for their work in bringing this book to production. It has been a pleasure and a privilege to work with all of you.

Other titles in the Library of Modern Jewish Literature